In Search of the Red Slave

Shipwreck and Captivity in Madagascar

MIKE PARKER PEARSON
& KAREN GODDEN

SUTTON PUBLISHING

First published in the United Kingdom in 2002 by
Sutton Publishing Limited · Phoenix Mill
Thrupp · Stroud · Gloucestershire · GL5 2BU

British Library Cataloguing in Publication Data
A catalogue record for this book is available from the British Library.

ISBN 0-7509-2938-3

Typeset in 10.5/14pt Melior.
Typesetting and origination by
Sutton Publishing Limited.
Printed and bound in England by
J.H. Haynes & Co. Ltd, Sparkford.

Contents

Acknowledgements

The story of Robert Drury was unravelled thanks to the hard work of Ramilisonina, Retsihisatse, Jean-Luc Schwenninger, Helen Smith, Victor Razanatovo and Georges Heurtebize: their fortitude, perseverance and unfailing good humour under the most trying of circumstances have made this book possible. We all owe a particular debt to Georges who not only worked with the project team whenever possible but also guided us through the history and culture of the Tandroy with great patience. Georges's own work provided the basis for much of our research and we are grateful for his help throughout the project.

Jean-Aimé Rakotoarisoa, Chantal Radimilahy and their colleagues at the Musée d'Art et d'Archéologie and Centre d'Archéologie at the University of Antananarivo have provided essential support and advice, as have Henry T. Wright, John Mack and other referees. We would never have got to Androy without their help. David Burney supplied information on megafaunal extinctions, Sarah Fee, Karen Middleton and Bram Tucker have shared their ethnographic expertise and insights with us, and Alison Jolly has been a voice of encouragement and enthusiasm since our first meeting. In Fort Dauphin, M. de Heaulme kindly allowed us easy access to Berenty and Trañovato. In England, Jeremy Viewing provided vital help with Landrover engines and spare parts.

We are especially grateful to Claude Allibert for his interest in our project and wish also to acknowledge the essential work of Pierre Vérin and René Battistini in establishing the basis of the archaeology of Androy. We thank Bill Fraser for his entirely unexpected interest in pirates which led us to much new information, and Arne Bialuschewski for the copy of his paper on pirates. Collin Carpenter identified the cannon and Ranald Clouston provided information on ships' bells. In the middle of her own research on Madagascar, Zoë Crossland found time to read the manuscript and Brian Boyd examined the excavated animal bone.

Mike wishes to thank Jim Symonds, Simon Garrod, Chris Clark and other colleagues in the Departments of Archaeology and Prehistory and Geography at the University of Sheffield and elsewhere for their interest in the Androy Project and its results. Irene de Luis de la Cruz and Rob Craigie drew the maps. The project was funded by the British Academy, the Society of Antiquaries, NERC, the Nuffield Foundation and the National Geographic Society. Clare Jackson at Sutton Publishing provided many editorial comments and brought the book to publication.

Our hosts and guides in Androy are, of course, too numerous too mention. Thanks go above all to the people of Ambaro, Androtsy, Ankiliabo, Laparoy, Montefeno, Taranake and Talaky for their kindness and hospitality during our long stays in their villages. We are grateful to our friends in Analamahery – especially Retsihisatse's wives and brothers – for their easy acceptance of our strange interests.

The transliterations of the names of many of the Malagasy kings in Robert Drury's story are those of Anne Molet-Sauvaget, whose 1992 translation into French of *Robert Drury's Journal* has been an important source for this book.

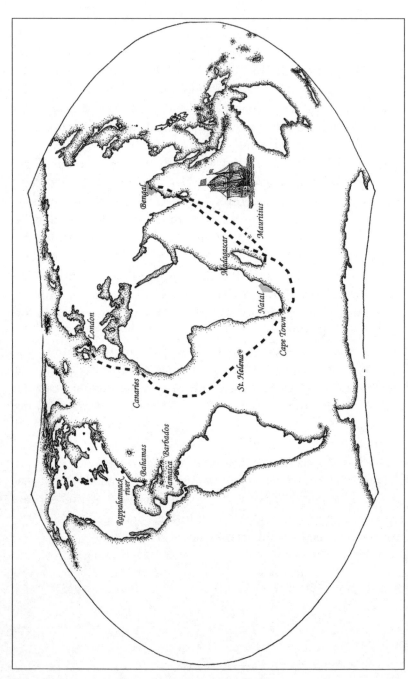

The voyage of the *Degrave* to India and Madagascar, 1701–3. Places visited by Robert Drury on later voyages are also shown.

The Pirates of Madagascar

Stealing someone else's ship on the high seas was once not only legal but positively encouraged. Europe in the seventeenth and eighteenth centuries was plagued by intermittent wars between the great powers as Spain and the Low Countries, Britain and France made alliances, changed sides, supported and confronted one another. Pitched battles and minor skirmishes changed the map of the world, and the land war was also a war at sea which made little distinction between civilians and combatants. In times of war armed merchant ships were authorised by government edict to seize any shipping and cargoes they found sailing under an enemy flag – privateering was considered one of the benefits of war.

But in the latter half of the 1600s privateering in the Caribbean exploded out of control. However much governments back in Europe, half a world away, insisted on the difference between the spoils of war and outright thieving, the potential profit from taking a ship at sea was worth the risk even in peacetime. The Caribbean had always offered rich pickings. From their mines in the Americas the Spanish shipped out immense quantities of silver aboard their treasure fleet, sending the wealth of the new continent home across the Atlantic to enrich the Spanish state. French and English ships conducted a brisk trade with their island colonies and the American settlers sailed south to do business with the Caribbean plantations. It was a lucrative spot in which to take up a life of crime.

The first buccaneers of the West Indies, mostly French with some English, had initially come together around 1630,

settling on the little island of Tortuga. No ship can stay at sea
indefinitely and pirates have always had bases on land, in
secret corners shielded from prying eyes. These men had lived
by hunting feral cattle, the descendants of animals left behind
on the islands by early Spanish explorers, and were named
after the *boucan*, a wooden grill used for drying meat. They
were eventually ejected for piracy by the Spanish and then
served as quasi-mercenaries for the English in Jamaica and for
the French on Hispaniola, fighting both the Spanish and the
Dutch. Once peace broke out, the buccaneers felt free to attack
and loot ships of any nationality.

But the governments of Europe had eventually had more
than enough of their depredations. The French and English
authorities set to. By closing down buccaneer bases in the
Caribbean, they scattered the lawless sea rovers around the
world. An act of God in 1692 helped sort out the problem –
Port Royal, the buccaneer haven on Jamaica, disappeared
beneath the sea in a convenient earthquake.

Living on their wits, the pirates always seemed to know
where to find a good haul. The Indian Ocean was just crying
out to be plundered. Since the early 1600s the English and
Dutch East India Companies had been exploring the trade
networks in the eastern seas and by the 1680s huge and
expensive cargoes – at least twenty a year to Britain alone –
were being sailed back and forth across a very empty ocean.
Although the East Indiamen carried cannon to defend
themselves, there was absolutely no naval presence in the seas
of India and Arabia. With no risk of having to take on a heavily
armed man-of-war, the pirates were on to a winner.

What was more, the first pirates to try their hand in the
Indian Ocean literally couldn't get themselves arrested. Until
1686 the East India Company authorities had no power at all
to try prisoners for piracy, and even after that date the courts
in India were remarkably lenient. The worst outcome for
captured pirates was to be sent back to England for trial, but
once there the courts needed evidence that piracy had indeed
been committed. Given that the scene of the crime was

thousands of miles away and, with any luck for the prisoners, the witnesses might be lost, dead or unreliable, there was always a chance of acquittal if all the accused kept their mouths shut. Many freebooters did hang but, in a dangerous and uncertain world, piracy was well worth the gamble.

Pirates arrived in the Indian Ocean in large numbers in the 1690s. It was not just the European shipping which drew them there. They were after even richer and more vulnerable quarry. Much of the Indian subcontinent was controlled by the Moghul Empire, ruled by Emperor Aurangzeb. This great Islamic empire was founded by descendants of Genghis Khan and Tamerlane (Marlowe's *Tamburlaine the Great*), who had invaded from Turkestan around 1527, and its power had been consolidated by forceful, clever rulers like Akbar and Shah Jahan. The latter had stamped the Moghul presence on northern India in the form of magnificent palaces, royal forts, mosques and monuments like the Taj Mahal.

Aurangzeb, Shah Jahan's son, had succeeded to the throne by imprisoning his own father in his palace at Agra, declaring himself *Alamgir*, Conqueror of the World. Under Aurangzeb's rule, the empire expanded to the widest extent it ever knew. The courtly elite lived an extravagant life, with the best in local and imported luxuries – food and spices, armour and weapons, textiles and carpets, jewels and ornaments. This wealthy empire traded far and wide, by land and sea. An important component of the maritime trade was between Gujarat in the far north-west of India and the ports of Arabia and the Horn of Africa. Gujarat supplied cottons and silks to the Persian Gulf as well as to Sumatra and Java, receiving spices, sandalwood and tin in return. Geography contributed to the region's economic success – it not only had access to the shipping lanes but it also lay close to the caravan routes to Delhi and northern India, and thence to the Great Wall of China in the east, and the routes via Aleppo and Damascus to the Mediterranean and the west. At the close of the seventeenth century the Moghul Empire had governed Gujarat for over a hundred years and brought peace to its hinterland, subduing outlaw bands and local potentates in return for a substantial revenue extracted from its traders.

The Gujarati traders were a very mixed community of Hindus, Moslems, Parsis, Jains and Europeans. The Moslems owned and sailed most of the shipping to the ports of Arabia and the Hindus dominated the brokerage, money-lending and commercial transactions. The Parsis were renowned ship-builders and victuallers of ships, while some of the Jains were jewellers, dealing in pearls and precious stones. The merchants of Gujarat sailed the entire Indian Ocean and could be found in almost every trading emporium from Kilwa on the African coast to Siam and Java in the distant east. The port of Surat in Gujarat, where the East India Company had a base, had grown into a city, swollen each year by the influx of Moslem pilgrims making the *hajj* to Mecca by sea.

The wealth of their cargoes made Gujarati ships sailing between India and the Persian Gulf a prime target for attack. Local pirates had been a danger to shipping in this region for centuries, preying on the Arab dhows and Indian merchant vessels that caught the seasonal monsoon winds to voyage back and forth across the Arabian Sea, and from the late 1680s European and American pirates were active in these sea lanes. In 1689 one Dutch and two English ships were reported at rest in St Augustine's Bay, in south-west Madagascar, 'richly laden with stores of silk' that they had stolen from a ship trading between Surat and the port of Mocha in Arabia. Even their sails were repaired with the looted silk. From the little island of Ile Sainte Marie off Madagascar's east coast the *Batchelor's Delight* out of Carolina had raided Indian shipping in the Red Sea in 1691.

In 1695 Captain Henry Avery – also known as John Avery, Long Ben or Captain Bridgeman, whom Daniel Defoe called the 'King of the Pirates' – captured the mighty treasure-ship *Gang-i-Sawai*, owned by Aurangzeb himself. It was carrying not only some wonderful loot but also pilgrims returning from the *hajj*. Avery's men tortured the passengers to extract their valuables and raped some of the women – others jumped

The island of Madagascar, showing places mentioned in the text. Pirate bases are marked with a skull and crossbones.

overboard to avoid this fate. Avery himself boasted of securing from this ship a Moghul princess to be his wife, but all the records indicate that the unfortunate girl he captured was merely an attendant of a rather elderly royal relative. In the Hollywood version of this swashbuckling act of piracy, the princess is played as a pouting nymphet in diaphanous veils, eventually rescued by Errol Flynn from the fate worse than death.

The pirates' violent depredations enraged Aurangzeb and back in Britain the government realised that something had to be done. Rather than go to the expense of sending a Royal Navy squadron, they put the job out to contract. This was awarded to a somewhat dubious syndicate, a group of men, under the direction of the Governor of New York, who were deeply involved in the slave trade. Needing someone tough and trustworthy to head the pirate hunt, the syndicate made a startling appointment – Captain William Kidd.

In his fast and heavily armed ship the *Adventure Galley*, Captain Kidd set off from New York to the Indian Ocean in September 1696, armed with a commission bearing the Great Seal of England which enjoined him to apprehend any pirates he came across. But Captain Kidd was soon showing the other pirates how to do it by taking his own prizes, capturing several Indian ships in 1697 and the *Quedah Merchant* with its choice cargo in 1698.

Another rich *hajj* ship was taken that same year by Robert Culliford, a pirate operating out of Madagascar and a new henchman of Captain Kidd. The Cornishman Culliford and the Scotsman Kidd knew each other from years before – in 1690 Culliford had been a crewman on Kidd's old ship the *Blessed William*, a privateer in the West Indies. Their acquaintance-ship had got off to a bad start when Culliford seized Captain Kidd's ship from under him, leaving Kidd stranded ashore. Culliford's prize was the *Great Mohamet*, returning to Surat from Jeddah. She was sailing under the protection of an armed East Indiaman but was too far out in front of the convoy for safety. Three pirate ships forced her to surrender, murdering most of the crew, and torturing the captain, owner and merchants; they put 150 passengers into open boats without oars or provisions and kept 60 women for their own purposes. The pirates shared the booty, valued at £800 a head. A regular seaman's wages at that time were less than £24 a year so they were making a fortune.

Who crewed the pirate ships? Ordinary sailors for the most part, none of whom had set out to sea intending to be a pirate. It seems ships turned pirate if the captain and crew found themselves unable to resist the temptation of easy money. Captain Kidd himself argued to the end that he was no pirate and that his men had acted against his wishes. There were undoubtedly many unwilling pirates. Sailors on ships that fell into the hands of these predators of the oceans faced an unpleasant choice: death, marooning or continuing to work for the new regime. Ships often left behind some of their crew in foreign ports, particularly men who were too sick to travel when their ship was due to sail. These abandoned sailors faced possibly months of destitution in some pestilential harbour town and often chose to ship out on the next vessel that came by, pirate or not.

Some pirates may have been unwilling but for others it was a way of life, with more personal liberty than any other. In the West Indies convicts, escaped slaves, political exiles and religious radicals of many nationalities had sought their freedom. Such men were already outcasts and those who turned to a life of crime on the high seas chose to abandon their last links with normal society and their former lives, drowning their own pasts in a pirate identity. Pirates lived outside the bounds of nations and their brutal naval regimes. In some ways the Jolly Roger (from the French *jolie rouge*) with its skull and crossbones was not simply a warning of death to the enemy but also a self-identification: death, violence and limited time marked out these men 'numbred neither with the living nor the dead'. From the 1690s the ships of these pirates were, in the euphemism of the time, 'on the account' in the Indian Ocean, using Madagascar as their base.

Madagascar is the fourth largest island in the world. It is twice the size of the British Isles at 1,000 miles long and 300 miles wide. Lying 400 miles off the south-east coast of Africa, it is a country with an extraordinary diversity of environments, from deserts to rainforests to mountain plateaux, but its people have a distinct island-wide identity. The ancestors of today's Malagasy came from far away. Around two thousand years ago a series of migrations from Indonesia brought the first people to this uninhabited island. The voyage of the Indonesian explorers was one of the great migrations of history, a journey of at least 3,000 miles across the Indian Ocean in outrigger canoes. In recent years a group of Australians attempted to simulate this feat of navigation by building a giant outrigger and sailing it westwards from Indonesia, directly across the vast and empty expanse of ocean. Safeguarded by modern communications and rescue services, they successfully made the crossing (although only just), showing that it would indeed have been possible. Yet there was no need for the emigrating people from south-east Asia to build outsized canoes or to sail straight across those dangerous seas, heading off into nowhere in the hope that there might be land out there somewhere. Far more likely is the scenario of long-distance land-hopping around the northern edge of the Indian Ocean, breaking the journey by clinging to the coasts of Sumatra, Sri Lanka, Arabia and East Africa.

After its settlement by the Indonesian migrants Madagascar did not long remain an isolated place, remote from the rest of the world. For hundreds of years before the pirates arrived ancient trade routes had stretched across the southern oceans. Madagascar was part of a giant commercial network which spread its web across the entire Indian Ocean and reached as far as the Mediterranean, a network into which Europe introduced itself only in the sixteenth century.

Even in the days of the Roman empire goods and products were traded over extraordinary distances. Archaeologists have found remains of Roman imports as far away as Sri Lanka and even on the East African mainland, just 400 miles across the

Mozambique Channel from Madagascar. The Romans even had a travel guide, the *Periplus of the Erythrean Sea*, written in the first or second century AD, for the use of merchants sailing from Egypt into the Indian Ocean. It details the route all the way down the African coast to the lost port of Rhapta (which is thought to be in modern-day Tanzania), but Madagascar lay undiscovered, beyond the knowledge of the classical world.

For centuries Arabs dominated the trade in the Indian Ocean and the first descriptions of Madagascar were written by Arab geographers nearly a thousand years ago. They refer to mysterious places called Wakwak, Kumr and Buki, names the Arab explorers gave to the new-found lands of Madagascar, the Comoro Islands to its north, and their peoples. From East Africa and Arabia a new wave of migrants sailed to the great island, arriving between six hundred and three hundred years before the pirates.

Influencing the island's earliest way of life, derived from the prehistoric Indonesians and Africans who had first settled an entirely empty land, these newcomers imbued Madagascar with their Islamic culture. In the north-west of the island they established small towns and ports, and in the south-east ritual specialists still pass down through the generations a secret Arabic writing known as the *sorabe* ('big writing').

Between 1405 and 1433 another nation's explorers ventured into the Indian Ocean. A great Chinese admiral, the eunuch Cheng Ho, led seven expeditions out of the distant east, the greatest comprising over three hundred ships and nearly twenty-eight thousand men. The largest of his ships were enormous, some as much as 300ft feet long. The last three of his expeditions reached the African coast, getting as far south as Mogadishu and Malindi, in voyages covering over 7,000 sea miles on the outward leg alone. The scale of such journeys dwarfs the subsequent crossings of the Atlantic by Columbus and other European adventurers.

The Chinese managed to miss Madagascar, but there were certainly contacts between the great island and the African coast. Along with an Indonesian heritage, there is also a strong

African influence in Madagascar. Unlike the light-skinned rice-cultivators of the central highlands, the Sakalava people of the west and the cattle-herding Tandroy people of the south look more like East Africans than Indonesians. Along the humid east coast, many small tribes with some African ancestry inhabited the narrow coastal strip between the escarpment of Madagascar's highland plateau and the shores of the Indian Ocean.

Here pirates colonised the island of Ile Sainte Marie. Lying 9 miles off the east coast of Madagascar, this 26-mile-long island only 3 miles wide was a perfect hide-out. Vessels could be concealed on its west coast in a natural harbour, hidden by the island's hills, where they lay in wait for the shipping that sailed past Madagascar's east coast. Pirates called in to repair their ships and find some rest and relaxation. There was even a local shop, supplied from New York, which stocked hardware and items such as hats and garden seeds (and rum, of course). From this haven some men took the opportunity to write letters home to their wives, to be delivered by any ship heading back to the Americas. Others went into retirement, settling down with local women for a quiet life as farmers. Relations with the locals on Ile Sainte Marie and the neighbouring coast were not easy and the pirate settlements were troubled by internal dissension and native attacks. The pirates built defences around their little colonies and by 1698 one group had built a fort defended by cannon.

Pirate settlements sprang up elsewhere in Madagascar: in the south-west the port of St Augustine sheltered many and in the north-west yet more were working out of Massalege, near an ancient port established by Arab traders centuries before. According to *A General History of the Robberies and Murders of the Most Notorious Pyrates*, published in 1724 by Captain Charles Johnson (who may have been Daniel Defoe writing under one of his many pseudonyms), some of these outlaws of the sea ended up on the island's northernmost peninsula. Here in the bay of Diego Suarez, they founded a Utopian socialist republic named Libertalia. Today there is a Malagasy restaurant in Diego Suarez called 'Libertalia' but no more tangible sign of the two great 40-gun forts that the pirates are supposed to have constructed there.

Any merchantman sailing into Malagasy waters knew that pirates were a real threat, although by 1700 some of the more notorious crews had departed. Kidd's associate Culliford and fourteen of his crew from the *Mocha* surrendered to the British during an extended amnesty. Their promise of a pardon was betrayed when all but Culliford were hanged at Execution Dock, just above the low-tide mark at Wapping on the River Thames, their bodies being exhibited in chains on the riverbank. Culliford himself was tried at the Old Bailey in May 1701 and reprieved.

Captain Kidd was not so lucky. In 1699 he sailed back to America, where his wife Sarah was waiting for him. Sarah Kidd is said to have been a lovely woman. She married William in 1691; although she must have been years younger than her groom, she had already buried two husbands. Sarah was soon to be a widow again. Kidd was arrested in Boston and, although extradition for piracy was technically illegal, he was sent back to England for trial. At Execution Dock, on 23 May 1700, at the age of fifty-five, he was hanged – twice. The rope broke the first time, but not the second. He was drunk for the first attempt but had sobered up for his last breath.

Captain Kidd was executed for murder, having been found guilty of killing one William Moore, a gunner on the *Adventure Galley* whom he had hit over the head with a bucket. Most of Kidd's crew were either pardoned for turning king's evidence or reprieved after being sentenced to death for piracy. Although Kidd's booty was confiscated, his wife managed to hold on to what she claimed were her own possessions and soon married a fourth husband.

Kidd and Culliford had gone by the turn of the century but there were still plenty of pirates in Madagascar. Most steered clear of the southern coast, the land of Androy with its hazardous reefs, lack of harbours and unfriendly natives, but on the very south-east tip of this great island, in the country of the Tanosy people, a pirate king reigned supreme.

Abraham Samuells, a black native of Martinique in the West Indies, had shipped out of Boston in 1695 as quartermaster on the *John and Rebecca*, a New England ship captained by John Hoare. Ostensibly bound for the Guinea coast of West Africa, the *John and Rebecca* had promptly turned pirate and gone off to Madagascar. The ship called first at St Augustine, the pirate and merchant base on the south-west coast, near the modern town of Tuléar. Captain Hoare had then sailed to the pirate haven of Ile Sainte Marie. Fever there had killed many of the crew, including Hoare, so Samuells assumed command. They had had very poor luck as pirates so Samuells decided to take the remnants of the crew back to the healthier climate of America. Around August or September 1697 they anchored in the natural harbour of Madagascar's most southerly port, now called Fort Dauphin, intending to take on provisions for the long voyage home. Their ship was wrecked by a sudden storm but most of the crew made it ashore, where a peculiar turn of events changed their lives.

Fort Dauphin had once been inhabited by the French, in an attempt to establish a trading colony in Madagascar. They persevered for over thirty years until giving up the struggle in the face of war and disease, finally abandoning the place in 1674. When Abraham Samuells washed ashore over twenty years later, an elderly princess of the Tanosy people spotted a birthmark under his left breast. She promptly claimed him as her long-lost son, last seen in 1674 when he had been taken away by his French father. Her assertion was supported by one of the local factions.

For the next eleven years Samuells made the most of his luck. As King Samuel he ruled the kingdom of Anosy, displacing the reigning king and continuing his piratical ways. A visiting French sailor once threatened to expose Abraham Samuells as an impostor to his Tanosy subjects. The man was immediately shot and it is probable that the entire crew of his ship were massacred to protect Samuells' new identity.

Ships often called at Fort Dauphin to take on provisions and to barter for slaves. King Samuel taxed each of them £100 for the privilege (and issued official receipts) but he and his henchmen also worked out ruses to capture visiting ships, sneaking up on them in the night in canoes filled with armed Tanosy warriors. Such tricks certainly paid off and King Samuel thrived. When the Welsh pirate Evan Johns captured the American *Prophet Daniel*, he gave it to King Samuel as a gift, keeping the cargo as his own share of the takings. King Samuel sold on the stolen ship for 14,000 pieces-of-eight. The bill of sale, dated 31 October 1699, still survives and describes Samuells as 'Andian'Telenara' (*roandrian'ny Taoalanara* or 'king of Fort Dauphin').

2

Robert Drury Goes to Sea

The pirates had been lured to the Indian Ocean by a taste for adventure combined with greed. India was a source of wealth beyond the reach of the ordinary working man in England. To get a share of those riches entailed huge risks. The pirates gambled everything on their prowess as seamen and fighters – in other words they stole to get their share. Other men chose a more respectable and supposedly less hazardous route to fame and fortune, signing on with the East India Company.

It was one of the key commercial institutions of the day, 'a corporation of men with long heads and deep purses', according to the eighteenth-century writer and publican Ned Ward. The Company was founded in 1601 and had a legal monopoly on trade with the East. Its investors made spectacular amounts of money in the import–export business but by the 1690s trouble was looming. The Company's practices of bribery and corruption – the king's closest advisers sometimes received backhanders of £50,000 – had become apparent to Parliament.

In 1698 a rival company was floated to end the monopoly: the English East India Company Trading to the East Indies was bankrolled by rich Whigs, who were firmly opposed to the Tories who controlled the existing company. The king was in favour as the crown needed a source of funds to raise money for a war against the French and the Whig magnates behind the New Company tempted him with a bigger loan than that offered by the Tories. Yet the Old Company, given ample time to wind up, continued trading in the hope of undermining the New. The breaking of the trade monopoly could have proved devastating to profits. From the point of view of the investors, making big money in the early years of capitalism, it was fortunate that the competition between the two companies lasted only four years.

A boy named Robert Drury grew up in the shadow of this institution. It led him to a life not of wealth and adventure but slavery and loneliness, stranded thousands of miles from home. As a child, he had lived a stone's throw from the Old Company's offices in Leadenhall Street. The theatrical façade of this three-storey timber building must have been a magnet for small boys. At the top stood a large statue of a sailor flanked by two dolphins, above a mural of East India ships. Below this was the royal crest of arms, on top of the Company's crest on the first-floor balcony. Merchants and speculators crowded through the doors to attend the 'inch candle' auctions of the Company's imported goods, so called because each sale would last the time it took for a one-inch candle to burn out. Robert Drury would also have seen the Company ships on the Thames, flying their distinctive red-and-white striped flags.

Robert Drury – his name could also be spelled Drewry – was born around 20 July 1687 in the City of London, in Poor Jury Lane (today's Jewry Street), the northern part of the street of Crutched Friars. He was a true Cockney, born just ¾ mile from the church of St Mary-le-Bow. Robert's name and those of his parents, John and Mary Elizabeth, were written in the baptismal register of St Katherine Cree, a church which survived both the Great Fire of 1666 and the Blitz, and still stands on the north side of Leadenhall Street. The Drurys' first two babies, also called John and Mary, had died in April 1685 and February 1686. Robert, called Robin by his family, was the couple's first child to survive through infancy and was followed a year later by a sister Elizabeth. Another little John came and went, born in October 1690 and buried exactly one year later, but a third John survived, and was baptised on 3 January 1692.

Crutched Friars was one of the few districts within London's city walls untouched by the Great Fire. Here in the Middle Ages had stood a religious house providing alms for the poor and, at the time of Drury's birth, the area still retained its medieval character with timber houses and cramped alleyways. Elsewhere in the city the burnt-out areas were rebuilt by the turn of the century on a new plan of wide, straight streets. Public money was spent on the raising of imposing buildings like the Royal Exchange and the city's skyline was dominated by the forty-nine new churches designed by Christopher Wren.

The great dome of Wren's new cathedral was still unfinished in 1700 and the workmen on the scaffolding of St Paul's could see to the city's limits, marked by its dungheaps, and the green fields beyond. Although it was only 5 miles across and just over 2 miles from north to south, London, the city of trade, had spread beyond its ancient defences. Houses along the north bank of the Thames now stretched all the way to Westminster, the city of the royal court and government. Much of the old city did still survive. London Bridge, with its shops perched above the Thames, remained the city's only crossing point over the river and the Tower of London had also escaped the flames.

Both sides of the river eastwards were lined with wharves and watermen's stairs. The Thames was covered in boats, so crowded that many ocean-going merchant ships had to dock at Blackwall, 5 miles downstream from London Bridge and the heart of the city. A new suburb had grown up in Spitalfields, extending east into Bethnal Green and Whitechapel to create London's East End.

In 1690 the Drury family moved to Old Jury (Old Jewry, which runs north off Cheapside), a wide street of new buildings. Old Jury and Poor Jury Lane were names surviving from four hundred years earlier, when these streets had been inhabited by London's Jewry. The largest community of Jews in the country had once had a synagogue here but every one of them was expelled from England in 1290. The place names still survive today to mark their passing. Only about thirty years before Drury's birth, in Cromwell's time, were Jewish merchants allowed to return to Britain.

Old Jury was less than a mile from where the family had lived before, yet this part of the city was quite different, having been entirely rebuilt after the Great Fire. It was right in the heart of the city, with St Paul's to the west and the new financial institutions of the Bank of England and the embryonic stock exchange to the east. Here John Drury became the innkeeper of a pub called the King's Head. We know that this inn was a good-sized building since John Drury paid window tax on twenty windows at 6*d* each. It was a well-known tavern also known as the 'Beefstake House', a kind of Berni Inn of its day, frequented, so Robert Drury tells us in the account of his life written many years later, by 'Merchants, and other Gentlemen of the best Rank, and Character'. Little Robin's childhood was spent in earshot of traders who had wild tales to tell about the exotic places and peoples beyond the oceans and the huge fortunes that could be made there. Drury happened to be born right at the heart of an extraordinary boom in mercantile capitalism, at the nerve centre of a brave new world.

The Drurys were a well-to-do middle-class family. Robert's father was a freeman of the City of London, a member of the Worshipful Company of Innholders and a devout Anglican. He served as a churchwarden, which meant he was one of those responsible for administering relief to the poor of the parish, but in 1696 he got out of taking his turn as constable of the ward by paying the hefty fee of £9 in order to be excused the duty. Business at the King's Head must have been good because within ten years, in 1700, John Drury began investing in properties in the village of Stoke Newington, 3 miles to the north. The family moved out of the city to this rural suburb in 1701 or 1702. Elizabeth would have been nearly fourteen, little John only nine. Their elder brother did not go with them.

In 1701, at the tender age of thirteen, Robert Drury had left home. He was determined to go to sea, despite his parents' misgivings. He did not want a safe and short voyage, as they had tried to persuade him, but preferred the long haul to India where his cousin John Steel was employed by the New East

India Company. The Company ships had a fearsome reputation and many sailors died on board or during their stay in the Indies – but Drury was not to be put off. He must have been both astonishingly determined and painfully naïve. Young Robert got his parents' agreement somehow since, when he left, his father supplied him with provisions for the voyage and a trading cargo worth £100.

By 19 February 1701 Robert Drury was aboard the East Indiaman *Degrave*, setting sail under Captain William Young for the 'Coast and Bay' – the Coromandel coast and the Bay of Bengal on the east coast of India. Named after the family who co-owned her, the *Degrave* was one of the first ships chartered by the New Company and had already once made the round trip to the east, leaving London two years before to reach India in just five months. She had made the return voyage at the same excellent speed. One of the finest merchant ships of the day, she was a large vessel of 520 tons and armed like a warship with fifty-two cannon – most East Indiamen had no more than twenty-eight guns.

East Indiamen were superb ships, beautifully made and surprisingly fast, equalling the tea-clippers like the *Cutty Sark* of the nineteenth century. No plans have survived of the *Degrave* but she was probably built at Blackwall or Deptford. Building such a ship took over five hundred oak trees, each eighty to a hundred and twenty years old and weighing a ton. Massive stem- and stern-posts of oak were attached to the keel and the ship's frame was formed by a double layer of curved oak timbers – the skin of the ship – to which were fastened the floor timbers. The keel was made of elm because it survives better than oak underwater and the three masts were fashioned from immense Scandinavian pine trees.

The hull below the waterline was sheathed with slow-grown Baltic elm or oak to give it better protection against shipworm. This creature, *Teredo navalis*, is not actually a 'worm' but a burrowing mollusc which caused ships in tropical seas to have a use-life of only around four voyages. Rot was also a serious problem, especially in the parts of the ship washed by the sea and dried by the sun. It was countered by securing thick oak planking along the gunwales around the main deck and beech between the gunwales and the waterline. There was a floor immediately above the keel and, given the number of guns, the *Degrave* must have had two gun-decks below the open main-deck, each with barely 5ft headroom.

The *Degrave*'s muster-roll survives today. This list of the men serving aboard shows 52 officers and specialist crewmen, 50 ordinary seamen and 21 midshipmen. The first voyage to India had had a crew of 116, of whom 19 were sailing with Captain Young again on this second voyage. Young's son Nicholas was one of those coming back, promoted from ordinary seaman to second mate. This remarkable rise through the ranks reflected his father's influence rather than his own abilities, and it was to have catastrophic consequences later on the voyage.

The captain, some of the mates and the steward were Company servants but appointed and paid by the ship's actual owners – their salaries are not shown on the *Degrave*'s muster-roll. Captain Young's pay would have been about £10 per month, but he was expecting to make a fortune from side-deals on his private cargo and on the sale of Madeira wine in Bengal. He was already a wealthy man, owning not only a part share in the *Degrave* but also a new estate near Dover. The chief mate Charles Newton was paid £6 per month, although the remaining officers received less than £3 15s. Beneath the ship's mates and the steward in the pecking order were the boatswain, surgeon and gunner and the ship's craftsmen – the carpenter and the joiner, the cooper, the caulker and the sailmaker.

Lower down the list, paid less than £2 per month, were the smith, armourer, barber, tailor, cook and four 'musitioners' (the ship's band, who piped the captain aboard and played at formal occasions). Robert Drury and the other midshipmen aboard the *Degrave* were mere boys, going to sea to learn the trade and one day become officers. They probably earned nothing at all. Indeed, Drury's father actually had to pay for his passage – rather than letting him sign on as an ordinary sailor, young Robert's family were forking out to get him into the officer classes. He was under the care of the captain and officers while learning his duties and, since this was his first voyage, would have been referred to as a 'guinea pig'.

The midshipmen and the first to fifth mates were generally drawn from the gentlemanly classes, as were the surgeon, the chaplain and the captain's steward. The rest of the crew – the ordinary seamen – were no gentlemen but members of a notorious sub-culture.

With their distinctive rolling gait, sailors were easily recognisable on the streets of London, 'wild, staring, gamesome, uncouth animals' who hung around in the taverns of Wapping and in Southwark and other unpleasant slums south of the river. Seafarers were renowned for their constant bad language and their drunken and dissolute lifestyle while in port, 'ready to ride [a woman] in the open street . . . never at ease till they've received their pay, and then never satisfied till they have spent it'. Their faces were tanned and wrinkled, their forearms tattooed using ink or gunpowder, and their hands often scarred from shipboard injuries. In an age before nautical uniforms, merchant seamen wore canvas jackets tarred to make them waterproof and their other clothes – striped waistcoats and knee-length petticoat-breeches – were often decorated with gaudy ribbons and braid. Many sailors came to London from places with strong seafaring traditions in Devon and the north. They generally considered themselves 'bred to the sea', following in their fathers' footsteps and only making the grade when they had completed an India or China voyage. This was a young man's profession: many of them died on the job and the survivors retired from the sea in their thirties or forties, taking up land-based trades.

These ordinary seamen were paid £1 2s a month, wage labourers of the sea equivalent to their rural counterparts. 'Absence pay' of an extra month's salary for every six months the ship was away was paid out to their next-of-kin in England but was sometimes held back for six months or more. It was not awarded at all if the ship were captured by pirates or the cargo did not return safely. In times of war some merchant seamen not only lost all their pay but ended up in the Royal Navy to boot – press-gangs regularly boarded returning East Indiamen when they anchored in the Downs, off the Kent coast south of the Thames estuary.

There was little for the ordinary seaman to gain financially. He might smuggle back a few trinkets but only the higher ranks were permitted private trade. Food ashore could be good at times but the diet at sea was not. Ship's biscuit (hard, flat bread baked twice) became infested with weevils. Salted beef and pork, known to the sailors as 'salt horse' and 'hard salt junk', rotted in its barrels in tropical conditions. From the cook's point of view, rancid meat could always be cheered up with vinegar. Other staples were dried fish, dried peas and beans, butter and cheese. Company ships did carry lemons and currants: these were known to be good foods for a sea voyage even though the actual link between scurvy and vitamin C was not yet understood – many thought that fresh meat was a good cure for the mysterious ailment.

Water for the journey was barrelled on board straight out of the filthy Thames. Containing the effluents of London, its foul taste persisted for most of the voyage but, as the muck in the barrels putrefied and released mineral salts, so the water became pure and sweet-tasting. Indeed, imported Thames water was much in demand among the Company's officers in India. More palatable were the 40 tons of beer and the ton or more of cider, brandy, wine and rum included in the ship's provisions. The captain, chief officers and passengers enjoyed better food – some livestock was even tethered on board – and the young Drury, as a gentleman midshipman, probably dined at the captain's table.

On 13 February 1701 the New Company's Court of Directors had signed the *Degrave*'s letters of dispatch, to sail with the first fair wind on a voyage to and from the East Indies, taking on wine at Madeira in the north Atlantic on the route south. On the return from India they would be calling at the Dutch colony at the Cape of Good Hope and then either the island of

St Helena or Ascension in the south Atlantic. The captain's orders also instructed him to 'cause Religious Worship to be observed Solemnly & Devoutly on ye Lord's Day'. As well as the ship's chaplain among the crew of 123 men there was another clergyman on board as a passenger, bound for India.

Anchored off Deal in the Downs on 19 February, the day of the *Degrave*'s departure, were the warships of Admiral John Benbow, one of the great heroes of his day. Many years later his name was used by Robert Louis Stevenson as the name of the inn in *Treasure Island*. Benbow had seen active service throughout the recent war with France and had completed a two-year tour of duty in the West Indies, where he was due to return in a few months. William Franklin, one of the men on the admiral's flagship HMS *Winchester*, recorded in his somewhat erratic spelling that day 'ye Degrafe to ye E Ingis Capt. Young Commdr' in conditions of 'Littell wind hase ffogge wether' (haze and foggy weather). On board the *Degrave* was Benbow's eldest boy John, fourth mate at just nineteen years old. The admiral almost certainly watched the *Degrave* sail away with his son; he would never see the young man again.

The *Degrave* would have dropped its pilot at Deal where it anchored briefly. This was a regular stop to take on the richer passengers. Among those boarding the *Degrave* were John Hall, a surgeon for the Bay, Samuel Blunt, a Company writer, and Samuel De Paz, a Jewish diamond merchant, together with his son and his servant John Lapee. Here on the Kent coast six lucky souls jumped ship, heading off with their two months' advance pay of £2 4s.

Either running away at Deal was a regular scam or these men genuinely lost their nerve. Life at sea was hard and hazardous and a substantial proportion of any crew bound for the east would not live long enough to make the round trip. Leaving aside the risk of piracy, the chances of the ship going down were about one in twenty and the rotting food combined with the tropical diseases rife at each port of call stacked the odds against a long and healthy life. The *Degrave* was to be no exception in this respect, with a mortality rate even before the final disaster struck that outstripped the average for the East Indies run of one dead out of every ten men.

We know no details about the *Degrave*'s voyage to India. The Company ships had a bad reputation for maltreatment of their men, resulting in numerous mutinies during the previous decade. The captain had the authority to imprison and even execute members of his crew. Stories abounded of shipboard cruelty: on board the *Diana* ten years before the captain had imprisoned his own officers, nailing them up in their cabins, and then systematically terrorised the crew. We do not know whether Young and his officers were cruel disciplinarians, resorting to floggings to control the men during the long months at sea, and can only guess at the treatment meted out to 'guinea pigs' by the more sadistic sailors. Perhaps, though, it was an unremarkable voyage. From other accounts of the period we can piece together something of the *Degrave*'s passage.

The *Degrave* was one of fourteen East India Company ships to leave London that year. The merchant ships of both England and Holland sailed to a seasonal schedule dictated by the wind systems of the Atlantic and the Indian Ocean: most East Indiamen set to sea in February and March. From early September the ship's mates and the boatswain arranged the loading of the vessel, with lighters bringing supplies up and down the Thames, initially taking on at Deptford the armaments, timber, ropes, canvas, pitch, sheet lead, coal and other supplies essential for life at sea. Food, drink and cargo were brought on board later when the ship was moored further downstream at Gravesend prior to sailing. It was at Gravesend, on the north Kent coast, that the crew had gone aboard the *Degrave* in early February.

About a month after leaving London the East Indiamen had moved from the cold northern winter to the warm temperatures of Madeira. The *Degrave* spent a week in Madeira – years later Drury remembered it wrongly as the Canaries – and sailed on, picking up the north-east trade wind towards the Equator where virgin line-crossers might be ducked from the yard-arm if they failed to pay the traditional forfeit of a bottle of brandy. The route to India was not down the western coast of Africa but involved a long haul across the Atlantic on the north-east winds, towards South America. When the Brazilian coast became visible, ships went about towards the south-east, tacking against the south-east tradewinds to take them back across the south Atlantic to Africa. By late May the *Degrave* was rounding the Cape of Good Hope, the southernmost tip of Africa. She then sailed north-east, passing to the east of Madagascar with the winds of the south-west monsoon blowing her towards India.

Navigation was still an imprecise art. A book of charts called *Oriental Navigation* was to be published by a Company employee in 1703 but before that date charts of the Indian Ocean had no soundings and only marked simple outlines of coasts and a few place names. Latitude was estimated using a back-staff, measuring the sun's altitude at midday and avoiding the glare by having one's back to the light. No method to calculate longitude had yet been devised (John Harrison, who invented the chronometer, was only a boy of eight in 1701): to find a particular port ships sailed to the right latitude and then headed due east or west as required.

The *Degrave* had the good fortune to meet no pirates and on the evening of 21 June 1701 she reached Fort St George at Madras, on India's east coast, without any apparent mishap in the very fast time of just four months at sea. Fort St George belonged to the competition, the Old Company, and so Captain Young sailed on northwards, finally anchoring about 6 miles off Madapollam on 27 June. Here De Paz the jeweller and some of the other passengers were being rowed ashore in the ship's barge when the first disaster struck.

3

Death in India

At 8 o'clock that night the men on watch on the *Degrave* heard someone in the water calling out to them. Ordinary seaman Joseph Chamberlain was found clinging to an oar: the barge had capsized in heavy seas when it reached the coastal sand bar. Being a strong swimmer Chamberlain had headed back towards the ship but had seen no other survivors. The other fourteen men on the barge were presumed lost, including Samuel De Paz (who had been carrying about £1,000-worth of valuables) and his son. Of the crew, the names of seamen Ralph Lewis, William Stafford, William Spark, Patrick Carmichael and James Barbett are recorded in the *Degrave's* ledger as having drowned.

The ship stayed on the east coast of India for several weeks and then set sail again. On 31 July, some 600 miles further north, she entered one of the mouths of the Ganges and here Drury's cousin, John Steel, came aboard to pilot the *Degrave* through the sandbanks and mangrove swamps. The ship struggled through the giant waves where the current of the sacred river entered the Bay of Bengal, over the Braces, into the New Deep and upriver past the base of the Old Company (the site of the future great city of Calcutta), past the French *Compagnie des Indes* at Chandannagar and past the Dutch East India Company's establishment at Chinsura. On 11 August, 150 miles inland from the mouth of the Ganges, the *Degrave* finally reached a flat landscape of rice fields and coconut trees; here at Hugli, a town which took its name from the river on which it lay, was the New Company's base.

Drury's father had asked Captain Young to judge whether his cousin Steel appeared suitably able and honest to look after the boy and his cargo. The captain evidently considered he was not. He refused to let Drury disembark with Steel, instead taking it upon himself to trade in the boy's cargo for 'commodities of the country'. William Young probably had good reason not to trust the man. Steel had worked for the Old Company for sixteen years and was a skilful pilot, but three years before he had been up on a charge of piracy before an Admiralty court in London. Acquitted through a lack of evidence, he had been snapped up by the New Company as one of the few pilots who knew the treacherous waters of the Hugli river.

The two English East India Companies had employees in both London and India, stationed at either end of their connection to the trade networks which converged on the Indian Ocean. As well as skilled men like pilots, there were Company officials whose job it was to trade the cargo imported from England. Filling the *Degrave*'s hold were broadcloth (woollen cloth over a yard and a quarter wide) and silver, along with iron and other metals as ballast cargo. It may sound absurd to try to sell thick, heavy wool in a hot country but the East India Companies knew their market: English broadcloth was popular in India for use in slippers, cloaks, carpets and wall-hangings, and for saddle covers and palanquin linings.

Bringing into India the goods which were destined to leave on the maritime link back to Europe and the Americas were the busy sea routes from Arabia, as well as caravan trains which traded all the way from China. From the Red Sea came coffee and pearls. The Persian Gulf produced thoroughbred horses, silk and dates. India itself supplied diamonds and timber, as well as textiles – the most sought-after goods. India was the world's largest manufacturer of cloth and the market was hungry for cotton, not only for Europe but also to clothe the slaves working the New World plantations and to trade with the slaving kingdoms of West Africa.

Further east Java and Sumatra exported gold and pepper. The Dutch were acquiring nutmeg, cloves and mace from the

Spice Islands, where the Chinese could purchase delicacies such as edible birds' nests and sea cucumbers. In faraway China in the enormous ports of Canton and Macao, both bigger than London, Europeans were trading for tea, silk, porcelain and gold. Unfortunately the Chinese were not impressed with European goods and considered that the foreign merchants had little to offer them, apart from silver. Massive cargoes of silver were making their way from the Spanish and Portuguese mines in the Americas via Europe to India and China, some £400,000-worth being shipped annually to the Indies by the English East India Companies. Over a century later the British finally hit on a product that would tempt the Chinese: these picky customers began exchanging their accumulated silver for the opium brought to China in vast quantities by the British.

When the *Degrave* arrived in India in 1701 the recent history of the English enclaves had not been tranquil. Some of the Company's first trading posts in India had grown into major towns. Bombay, for example, was in English hands – the Portuguese had given it to Charles II as a wedding present and the crown rented it to the Company for £10 a year. The city had a mixed population of some sixty thousand people, Indian, British and Portuguese, living under a British administration. There were a lot of English residents in the territory of the Moghul Empire, but they were lucky still to be there on the Hugli, at Masulipatam and Madras further south on the Coromandel coast, and at Bombay and Surat on the west coast. Although Emperor Aurangzeb granted European merchants the right to trade in his domains in return for the revenues they brought in, relations between the foreigners and the Moghul Empire were often strained to breaking point.

In 1686 the English had embarked on an absurd war, pitting their tiny forces against the Moghul's hundred thousand-strong army. The 'invading' English had been forced to retreat from the Hugli even though their opponents, on account of the trade, were trying to make them see sense, make peace and stay. In 1689 the humiliated English had eventually proffered abject apologies and financial compensation to Aurangzeb.

In 1696 a rebellion by native rulers against the Moghul Empire had broken out in north-east India, threatening European interests on the Hugli, but it was over by 1698 when the rebel strongholds were destroyed by Aurangzeb's local governor. Since then the French, the Dutch and the English Old Company had each built a fortified base known as a 'factory' along the River Hugli; the names of Fort Orléans, Fort Gustavus and Fort William celebrated the reigning monarchs of Europe. The New Company's factory at the town of Hugli had no defences – one of the circumstances that would lead the *Degrave* and Robert Drury to eventual disaster.

Business here in north-east India was centred on cotton. Bengal produced the best textiles in the whole world – a huge range of muslins, calicos, taffetas, ginghams, seersuckers and chintz. The English conducted their transactions through a broker and intermediary merchants employed by the factory. The merchants bought the products of the local weavers, who were dispersed across an area of 1,000 square miles, and transported them to the Company's warehouses where the bales of cloth were graded by the chief sorter and his assistants.

Dispatched back to England on the returning Company ships, these foreign imports – worth £150,000 per year to the Company – were undermining the weavers of Spitalfields. Seeing their livelihood disappear, they had rioted in 1697 but had been pacified by an Act of Parliament passed in 1700. This forbade the importation of finished pieces, prohibiting the use or wearing in England of 'all wrought silks, Bengalls, and stuffs mixed with silk or herba, of the manufacture of Persia, China, or East India, and all calicoes painted, dyed, printed or stained there'. Heated arguments about the import and export of cloth were at the heart of the politics of international trade – it was a world of tariff barriers and vested interests trying to protect monopolies on the market.

Fabrics of all kinds, pepper and saltpetre would make up the bulk of the cargo to be sent back to England on the *Degrave*. Saltpetre, a constituent of gunpowder, made ideal ballast for ships, but its value was only high during wartime and, given that peace had recently broken out in Europe, the Bengal factory had been asked not to send home too large an amount. Opium was another popular commodity, along with products traded into Bengal from further afield, such as coloured woods, shellac (a resin produced by insects) and trinkets of many kinds.

The Moghul authorities kept out of the trade fight which had begun between the Old and New Companies in 1698, happy to take double the levy and bemused by this evidently insane commercial squabble. The confusion had provided an opportunity for Aurangzeb's government to lean on the English, to force them to do something to solve the problem of piracy in the shipping lanes between western India and Arabia. There were plenty of 'hat-men' – the English – at hand and Aurangzeb had threatened to kill the lot of them, starting by imprisoning every Englishman in Surat.

Fortunately he had also tried more conciliatory measures, putting pressure on the Dutch and English East India Companies to provide armed escorts for the Indian fleet's sailings to Mocha. To gain the emperor's favour, the New Company had agreed to police the seas against pirates. Unfortunately it had bitten off a lot more than it could chew: making war on such a slippery enemy was well beyond the Company's resources. Incensed by the lack of progress, the emperor threatened to withdraw English trading privileges. The promise to deal with the pirates was impossible to keep and the English hoped to fulfil their side of the bargain by merely agreeing to sail in convoy with the Indian ships. In the Moghul view this was quite inadequate and on 16 November 1701 the emperor finally lost patience and ordered all Europeans to be confined and their goods seized for failing to protect Indian shipping. In Bengal the Old Company was safe behind its walls at Fort William but the employees of the New Company were very vulnerable in their undefended factory at Hugli.

At this time, with a turbulent local situation becoming dangerous, the *Degrave* and her crew had been in India for four months already and now had to stay put much longer than the captain had intended. There is little information on how a merchant ship's crew passed these long periods in Bengal; together with daily tasks on board, there was shore leave, for the entertainments and amusements for which sailors around the world have always been renowned. The little midshipman Robert Drury was still just a boy of fourteen and the account of his adventures which he wrote over twenty-five years later tells us little about his stay in India other than that he learned to swim! Some evenings he would tie a rupee coin – worth 2*s* 6*d* – in a cotton sheet around his midriff and swim ashore with his friends for a night out.

The *Degrave* was made ready to return to London in the early months of 1702 and almost managed to get away. She actually set sail in March and was 60 miles down the Hugli when she was ordered back upriver to protect the New Company factory from attack by Indian forces. With her fifty-two guns she was effectively a well-armed artillery battery. In May the local political situation brightened, but globally it was a different story.

In late July a ship called the *Norris* arrived in Bengal with much news. The trade war was over – the rival companies had merged as the United Company of Merchants of England Trading to the East Indies. King William was dead, his sister-in-law Anne was queen and, when the *Norris* left England in March, war had been about to break out again. Although it was unknown to anyone in India for months to come, England had indeed declared war on France in May 1702. The *Norris*'s role in our story is very brief – shortly after reaching Bengal, she exploded and sank!

Month followed month and still the *Degrave* remained on defensive duties in the Hugli river. The best season to sail home came and went and the cargo was becoming damaged by rain seeping through the decks. The ship already had a reputation as a leaky vessel and by late October she was taking in an inch of water an hour. The real disaster at this moment was neither the conflict with the Moghul emperor nor the outbreak back in Europe of the War of the Spanish Succession but the deaths from fever here in Bengal. Drury's cousin, the pilot John Steel, had died in December 1701. There followed the deaths of at least forty of the ship's company. Most ominous for the future welfare of the *Degrave* and her crew were the deaths of the chief mate and of the captain himself. William Young died on 9 October 1702, leaving a decimated crew and an unseaworthy ship.

Young's son Nicholas, just twenty-five years old, was appointed captain by the Bengal Council with the admiral's son John Benbow promoted to second mate. Having buried his father, the new Captain Young bottled the dead man's heart so he might take it home for burial in England. The *Degrave* was prepared for departure, laden with a cargo of 130 bales of cloth, 50 tons of pepper, and more than 100 tons of saltpetre, with a total value of nearly half a million rupees – about £62,500.

The crew numbers were topped up to about 120 men. Sailors left behind when their own ships sailed provided a pool of stranded seafarers looking to work their passage home. So new seamen joined the ship, along with several passengers, including one James Wilcox being sent home for 'profligacy'. Of the two women passengers also on board one of them, Susanna Exeter, was already known to the crew of the *Degrave*. She had first come out to India as a passenger on their ship and was now being ordered home again for 'behaving lewdly'. None of the historical documents reveals exactly what Susanna had got up to! Another passenger, Samuel Conyers, had inherited a fortune and was going home to spend it – or so he thought.

The ship was declared ready. The young captain was warned by the Company to steer clear of the French and wait at the Cape (the Dutch colony which is now Cape Town) for a convoy to take them on the final leg. The *Degrave* sailed on 18 November 1702 under the charge of a river pilot who made a sorry mess of his job of guiding the ship through the Hugli's narrow channels. The *Degrave* touched bottom, damaged her rudder and either sprang a new leak or aggravated an old one.

On Christmas Day the *Degrave* dropped her pilot and headed out into the Bay of Bengal, leaking her way across the Indian Ocean. Robert Drury tells us that the crew had to keep two chain-pumps, each requiring a team of seven men, in continuous operation for the next six weeks. Taking in more and more water, the *Degrave* was forced to depart from its course to the Cape and head for the tiny island of Mauritius where the crew, exhausted from non-stop pumping, hoped that they could fix the leak.

The uninhabited island of Mauritius had been a refuelling stop for European ships since its discovery by the Portuguese in 1511. It was now occupied by the Dutch, who had been there on and off since 1638. That eponym for stupidity, ugliness and extinction, the dodo, was already on its way to posthumous fame, wiped out within fifty years of the Dutch arrival. Imported cattle, goats and rats were busily eating the crops grown by the Dutch and their slaves from the east coast of Madagascar. There were also runaway slaves living in the ebony-forested hills. The colony was not thriving but the Dutch were as helpful as they could be to the ship's weary crew, who erected a large tent on the shore and unloaded as much of the sodden cargo as was possible. For over a month the *Degrave*'s men worked on the hull but they failed to find the source of the leak.

Already on Mauritius when the *Degrave* arrived on 3 February 1703 were fifty Indian sailors, described by the island's Dutch governor as 'Lascars and Moors'. 'Lascar' comes from the Hindi and Persian word *lashkar* meaning army or camp and was a term used fairly broadly by the English in India to mean Bengali sailors, or Gujaratis, or the Portuguese-Indian people of the Malabar coast of the south-west.

Lascars had a poor reputation among the Europeans for being cowardly and prone to cold, useless on the rigging in a gale and the first to succumb to shipboard illness. Yet they were some of the most well-travelled sailors in the world, especially the Gujaratis, crewing for the largest shipping companies in existence. The group of men on Mauritius probably came from a ship owned by Abdul Gharfar, the greatest shipping magnate in Surat, who owned at least twenty vessels and managed a trading concern equal to both the English East India Companies together.

The lascars had been dumped on Mauritius two months earlier by a pirate, John Bowen, who had plundered their ship and taken them captive. Although Captain Bowen had then lost his own vessel, he and his crew had managed to disappear off to sea in a ship's longboat. The identity of these stranded lascars remains unknown but they had certainly been westward bound from India, probably from Gujarat, when their ship was taken. This was the season to sail towards the Gulf, catching the light winds and fine weather westwards that accompanied the north-east monsoon season from October to March.

The Gujarati sailors had little say in what happened to them next. The *Degrave*'s crew knew they would have to pump their way home and were anxious to recruit these men as extra hands and the Dutch were pleased to see them on their way – these uninvited visitors had been a drain on the little colony's food supplies. To leave Mauritius on the *Degrave* was the Indians' best chance of getting home: they would work their passage as far as the Cape and from there pick up a ship bound for Surat or Bombay.

As in India, men were regularly deposited on and picked up from Mauritius. Indeed, five men from the *Degrave* took the opportunity to spend a little longer in this island paradise and ran away into the hills, preferring to hide in the forest rather than risk death by drowning in a leaky tub. They emerged when the ship had left without them and were picked up six weeks later by a passing ship, the *Loyal Bliss*.

The *Degrave* should never have left Mauritius in the state she was in. The ship was too big to be careened (pulled ashore on to her side to be cleaned and recaulked) but she could have been emptied of her cargo, to be kept by the Dutch until another ship was sent to collect it. The inexperienced captain of the *Degrave* chose to leave behind just a single anchor, which was salvaged a month or so later by the *Nathaniel*, whose log recorded its provenance as 'Capt. Young from Bengall very leaky'. As the *Degrave* sailed away, despite all hands to the pump day and night, the water level was rising slowly in the ship's hold.

Young was all for keeping on course for the Cape but the crew realised that the ship would never stay afloat that long. When they reckoned they were 100 leagues (about 300 miles) from Madagascar's south coast they persuaded the captain to change course and head for the nearest land. Several cannon and 'heavy goods', probably the saltpetre, were heaved overboard to lighten the load. Three days later land was sighted.

One of the crew knew something of this part of Madagascar and its recent history. He recognised the distant promontory as Fort Dauphin, the failed French colony whose inhabitants had been massacred by the indigenous Tanosy in 1674. It was now under the control of the pirate king Abraham Samuells, who was, to quote Drury, 'an Enemy to all White Men, and treated all the Europeans in a most barbarous Manner'. Even though the English, the Tanosy and the pirates had a common enemy – a mutual fear and dislike of the French – it was decided that landing here might not be a terribly good idea. The inhabitants of Fort Dauphin had a fearful reputation and falling 'into the Hands of these revengeful, and bloody Murderers' was not a favoured option.

4

Shipwrecks and Scotsmen

We do not know where most of the young men whose ship was sinking on the shores of Madagascar had started their lives. They may have been city urchins or country boys who had gone to London to ship out with the merchant fleet. The pirate captains certainly came from a variety of places – some were born in the colonies, in America or the West Indies, but many came from the harbour towns of the West Country, Wales and Scotland. We do know that they had all experienced life in wartime – nine years of war against the French had only ended in 1697 and the peace was already over when the *Degrave* left India. Ruled by the 'Sun King' Louis XIV, the most powerful monarch of his day, France was the superpower of Europe. The wars against the French were partly motivated by suspicions that Louis planned to invade England and restore a Catholic sovereign. England was a Protestant nation which had expelled the Catholic James II in the Glorious Revolution of 1688 and crowned as monarchs James's elder daughter Mary and her husband and cousin, the Protestant Dutchman William of Orange. Religion and politics were closely intertwined and everybody hated the French.

This fear of both the bloodthirsty pirates and the old enemy, the French, meant the desperate men on the leaking *Degrave* dared not approach Fort Dauphin, but their ship was clearly not going to make it to the next port – St Augustine was still 400 miles away. The hold was half-full of water and the powder magazine, normally the driest part of the ship, had water 4ft deep in it. The ship would have to be grounded soon if she were not to sink in deep ocean.

They had passed the forested and rocky shores west of Fort Dauphin and were now sailing along a bleak coastline of wind-blasted scrub with an inshore reef against which the waves crashed and foamed. Coming in close, they finally spotted a possible landing site, 'a Sand which ran along for two Leagues'. The crew worked frantically: they let go one of the anchors, chopped down the masts, and jettisoned more of the cannon to keep afloat and get in as close as possible to the shallows. Men laboured through the night to construct a raft. On the morning of 27 April 1703 the chief mate and four men set off towards the shore in the *Degrave*'s only boat, dragging a long rope to set up a cable to tow the raft ashore.

They knew they had been spotted by local people watching from the sandy cliffs. The *Degrave*'s crew were about to enter the world of the Tandroy*. Their name means 'people of the land of thorns' and today they still live in the extreme south of Madagascar in the region called Androy, 'the land of thorns'. The thorns in question belong to a little tree (the *roy*) with wickedly sharp spines. The vegetation of Androy is extra-ordinary – the *roy* is just one of many prickly and poisonous trees and bushes which form the spiny forests of the arid south. Many species are unique to southern Madagascar and most striking are the *fantiolotse*, which grow in clumps of great coral-like fronds pointing skywards, covered in spines and tiny green leaves which taste of blackberries. Less common are baobabs and similar bottle-trees whose smooth grey bark stretches like skin around their spongy trunks. There are many different species of euphorbia, whose poisonous fleshy leaves are adapted to semi-desert conditions. In the rocky hills of northern Androy there are today remnants of great forests where lemurs, tortoises, tenrecs (spiny creatures like long-legged hedgehogs), wild cattle and wild boar once roamed.

The region controlled by the Tandroy in the early 1700s stretched about 50km inland from the coast on which Drury

* Pronounced Tan-drew-ee.

and his companions were attempting to land. On its east side their country was bounded by the Mandrare river while its western margins reached to just beyond the Manambovo river, a territory 100km across. Between the two rivers lay the heartland of Androy, a sandy plain enclosed by hills to the north and ancient sand dunes to the south.

On a latitude equivalent to that of Miami and Brisbane, Androy can be extremely hot, and in 1703 the climate was much the same as it is today. Before the onset of the rains there are many days in October and November when it feels too hot to move at all. Although the land of thorns has an annual rainfall equivalent to that of Paris, rain falls only in December, January and February, and the region suffers from crippling droughts. There are few watercourses anywhere in Androy and all of them dry up completely from May to November. Finding water in the dry season is desperate work – there are a handful of natural ponds but the Tandroy survive by digging deep into dry streambeds, looking for underground moisture.

When the *Degrave* arrived the human inhabitants of this arid place were probably fewer than forty thousand strong but had a reputation among neighbouring tribes as a fierce and tough people. We cannot say for certain where they came from or why they settled in the spiny forests rather than seeking out better-watered lands elsewhere on the sparsely populated island. Although the great migrations from Indonesia and Africa are too long ago to be remembered in oral histories, the Tandroy do have a number of myths about their arrival in the region. They know that in the distant past their ancestors came from over the seas. The Tandroy speak a dialect of a language common to the whole island which ultimately has its roots somewhere in Indonesia, being most similar to a language still spoken in Borneo. But many words come from Swahili, the trading language of the East African coast. No one knows what language was spoken by the forebears of the Tandroy. By the end of the seventeenth century the Malagasy language was already spoken all over the island and the Tandroy of the far south spoke a dialect of it.

The Tandroy say that their ancestors landed in the east, in the neighbouring region of Anosy. From there they walked into Androy and gave rise to a dynasty of kings, divided into a northern line and a southern line. Archaeology has given us a good idea of how long the land of Androy has been inhabited – there was absolutely nobody there before about AD 700, but a mysterious prehistoric culture had arisen by about 1200. The Tandroy and their kings were certainly in control of the region by the 1600s. During that century the inhabitants of southern Madagascar lived in a state of perpetual war. A new export from Europe – the gun – reached even this remote corner of the Indian Ocean and changed Malagasy society. First seen by the Tandroy some sixty years before the arrival of the *Degrave*, when the French colonists first arrived in Fort Dauphin, the musket had soon become a sought-after possession. The old matchlock, with its dodgy fuse liable to go out in wind or rain, had been superseded around 1690 by the sophisticated flintlock gun and the men waiting on the coast that April morning, watching the *Degrave*'s sailors struggling for their lives in the surf, were eager to acquire this new weapon.

Cattle were the Tandroy's link to the outside world. They could swap them for guns with their Tanosy neighbours, who in turn were trading with the Europeans who called at the little port of Fort Dauphin to exchange guns for slaves. In the early eighteenth century slavery was a fact of life throughout Madagascar, as was the warfare necessary to take captives. The Tandroy kept thousands of slaves, whom they normally acquired in battles with their neighbours. They were sandwiched between two powerful kingdoms: the Tanosy to the east were well armed but the bellicose Mahafaly to the west, cattle herders like the Tandroy, were greater in number. Conflicts over territory had always created slaves but contact with Europeans was causing an escalation in violence. The 'red foreigners' (white men, *vazaha mena* to the Malagasy) seemed keen to acquire as many slaves as the Tanosy could produce and the guns which they brought to Madagascar fuelled further warfare. In 1703 southern Madagascar was a violent and dangerous place. The Tandroy seized any chance to take prisoners and the men of the *Degrave* were going to be easy prey.

The little boat from the ship was dashed against the reef and the Tandroy gathering on the beach ran into the water to help pull the rope's end ashore. On the sinking *Degrave* about fifty people clambered on to the raft which they had built overnight and then hauled it along the hawser to get to the safety of dry land. But the raft too came to grief, capsizing and tipping everyone into the sea. One of the women passengers drowned in the surf. Aboard the *Degrave*, Captain Young realised that the only way for everyone else to reach the shore alive was to sail his distressed vessel straight on to the reef and disembark while it was smashing itself to pieces. The drastic plan worked – two men were drowned and several others had to be revived but otherwise all 170 or so made it safely to land and were soon drying out around a large fire. The captain swam ashore clutching the bottle containing his father's pickled heart, still hoping that he might take it home for burial in Dover.

Several hundred Tandroy had arrived. They made no threats to the Europeans, concentrating on picking over the calicos and silks washing up from the tons of cargo spilling from the *Degrave*'s hold. A cow was brought down to the seashore and slaughtered to feed the shipwrecked strangers, who were shocked by their first introduction to Tandroy cuisine: the fur and flesh were cooked together and the animal's guts were toasted directly in the ashes of the fire. After waiting on the beach for two days and nights, sleeping under bits of the cloth which had floated ashore, the crew were surprised by the arrival of a stranger, a young man who announced that he was an Englishman too, from Middlesex. His name was Sam and he had been shipwrecked here two months earlier, with a small band of Scotsmen. He told the new arrivals that the Tandroy king would be coming to see them the next day. The good news was that there was no need to be afraid. The bad news was that King Kirindra would not be letting them go.

Drury describes in detail their first encounter with the one-eyed king of the Tandroy. Kirindra arrived with a party of two hundred warriors armed with spears; he greeted the captain courteously and presented him with supplies of food and drink, including six calabashes of *toaka* (rum). The Europeans were then peremptorily notified that they would all be accompanying the king back to his capital, Fenoarivo. The crew's hope was that there they would meet the rest of Sam's party and together they might work out a solution to their predicament – how to escape.

Fenoarivo should have been only two days' walk from the coast but the crew took three. They were exhausted and many had been injured on the reef. Some had no shoes at all and most had 'but bad ones'. Along the narrow path from the sea thorn bushes shredded their clothes and by late morning their feet were scorched by the hot sand. The crew came across Tandroy villages that were entirely empty since the men had gone down to the sea to scavenge the ship's cargo and the women had run in fear into the woods. Later that day they took honey, milk and beef from a little group of 'hovels'. That night, stopping to kill and cook a bullock, they received their second culinary shock. This desert land had almost no water and what they did find Drury remembers as being 'very thick, and nasty . . . fetch'd at a great Distance out of Holes, and Pits in the Woods'. The meat that they ate for breakfast was full of sand.

The party had reached the forests of spiny trees and now those without shoes were 'sorely prick'd and hurt in the Woods'. On the third day's march young Robert Drury lost one of his purses, one of the few items other than his mother's 'medal' (perhaps a locket) that he had saved during the shipwreck. They marched further and faster that day and reached Fenoarivo at nightfall. Drury estimated that they had walked 50 miles – it may have felt like 50 to his tired feet and weary mind but they had actually covered only 30 miles in three days.

King Kirindra's capital was the principal of seven royal villages. Recently founded in an area of dense forest, it was protected by a palisade wall of trees – tall, thin and spiny *fantiolotse* grew so close together that they formed an impenetrable barrier. The village compound was about a mile in circumference with the fence of living trees enclosing a large clearing full of rectangular wooden houses, granaries and cattle pens. King Kirindra's residence was the largest building in Fenoarivo but was far from palatial, being only 14ft long and 12ft wide. Its walls of wood and dry grass supported a thatched roof and it had low and narrow doorways.

To Drury's eyes the royal court was a bit short on pomp and circumstance. This king not only lacked a throne, he didn't even have a chair. Kirindra and his queen sat cross-legged on mats which covered the hard-packed earth of the house floor. Drury soon discovered that although the unimpressive wooden houses seemed a bit on the small side, everyone – parents, children and slaves – cooked, ate and slept together on the mat-covered floor. As for possessions, even the nobility of the Tandroy had few, just calabashes for collecting water, earthenware pots and a variety of wooden tubs, platters and spoons.

The dress of the royal court was as simple as its architecture. Men wore a loincloth and wrapped themselves in a shawl or *lamba* of locally woven cotton, the universal garb of Madagascar. Women dressed most modestly, covered by a large *lamba* from the midriff to the feet, worn over a short-sleeved knee-length cotton shift. Some *lamba* worn by people of status were made of silk, either the coarse local product or from imported fabrics. The very poor made their *lamba* from the beaten-out pulp of tree bark. The men's oiled hair was elaborately tressed but the only female adornments Drury noticed were the beads of various colours which rich women sewed in geometric patterns on to their dark dresses. People of distinction also wore bracelets of copper or silver and, more rarely, of gold. For freeborn men spears and the few muskets that the Tandroy possessed were as much items of adornment as they were weapons.

Waiting in Fenoarivo were some glum faces – two unhappy Scotsmen named Robert Drummond and Alexander Stewart. These two sea captains belonged to the Darien Company, an ill-fated Scottish version of the East India Company. In the

closing years of the seventeenth century there had been no
love lost between the English and the Scots. Poor harvests
during the 1690s had led to terrible famine in Scotland but no
relief had been sent from English supplies. In 1698 five
Scottish ships had attempted to establish a colony at Darien in
Panama, but the English were forbidden to send supplies or
help to the two thousand people who died there from disease
and attacks by the Spanish. English investors were prevented
by law from having any involvement with the Darien
Company because it was considered to be aiding a foreign
power. Curiously, the Scots had not made the venture easy for
themselves as their trading cargoes of wigs and Bibles were not
exactly snapped up by the Panamanian Indians.

Drummond and Stewart had left Glasgow in the summer of
1701, heading not for Panama but for Africa. They had,
however, changed course to the Indian Ocean. Did they decide
to turn pirate and go 'on the account'? On Ile Sainte Marie they
had loaded slaves into their ships, the *Speedy Return* and the
Content, and in June 1702 had sailed to the island of Bourbon
(now called Réunion) to sell them to the French colonists
there. Drummond and Stewart had then headed for Matatana
on the east coast of mainland Madagascar, where they had
landed with a few of their crew to see what they could trade.
They should have been more careful – while they were ashore
pirates captured both their ships. The pirate captain was the
same John Bowen who had dumped the Gujarati sailors on
Mauritius. Bowen's piracy was responsible for the presence
here in Androy of two groups of people from very distant
countries and cultures.

Bowen and his men had sailed off in the Scottish *Speedy
Return* but soon burnt it after capturing a better ship. Pirates
had no sentimental affection for their ships – if their own
vessel was in poor condition or a bad sailor, they would
transfer all their men and property to the next good ship they
captured. Some of the men from the *Speedy Return* were still
alive, working alongside Bowen's pirate crew, when the ship
put in at Mauritius a year later in January 1704. Two of them

managed to escape there and were later picked up by a passing English vessel.

Although he took their ships, the pirate Bowen had left Drummond, Stewart and a few of their men with a longboat, and this little party had made plans to sail all the way around the south coast to St Augustine in the west. The young man named Sam had met the Scotsmen in Matatana where he had been stranded for months having gone ashore on sick leave from a pirate ship. He was not a pirate by choice but was simply staying alive – the merchant ship on which he was originally sailing to the East Indies had been captured by pirates. A Malagasy woman named Dudey and her English husband from Ile Sainte Marie were also with Sam at Matatana. This man may actually have been a pirate; Drury never names him and may have been discreetly protecting his identity.

The three of them had teamed up with the Scots and set off in the boat on the dangerous voyage to the west coast, only to be blown on to the Androy shore about 10 miles from the site of the *Degrave*'s wreck on the reef. After spending a fortnight in King Kirindra's capital the castaways had realised they were never going to be allowed to leave. One moonlit night they had tried to slip away from Fenoarivo but the Tandroy were expert trackers, easily following their shoeprints through the woods, and had soon caught up with them. The Europeans had made a stand, refusing to return to Fenoarivo, and had even shot and wounded one of the Tandroy. To no avail – they had been marched back to the angry Kirindra.

That was over two months ago. Now that Drummond's party had been joined by the crew of the *Degrave*, the shipwrecked foreigners had strength in numbers. Not wanting to live out the rest of their days as 'guests' who could never leave, the senior members of the two parties soon concocted an escape plan, spurred into swift action by a rumour that Kirindra was thinking of killing them all. They would take the king hostage and walk everyone out of Fenoarivo, heading for the frontier of the kingdom of Anosy beyond the River Mandrare to the east.

5

Slaughter and Survival

The first part of the plan went reasonably well. Early in the morning the captains calmly paid a visit to the king's house, where they seized him, his wife and his nephew. A stray pistol shot alerted the village, however, and the king's men moved to surround the escape party. In a brief skirmish, one of the crew was killed and three others were wounded. It was crucial now for the leaders to use all their knowledge and resources: the crew had plundered the village and found thirty guns, they had three valuable hostages and they had interpreters. Drummond's party had been marooned in Madagascar for nearly a year and so had acquired some knowledge of the language.

They informed King Kirindra that he would die on the spot if the Tandroy continued shooting. The threat worked: the king called on his men to cease fire and the crew began their march to freedom, deploying their meagre arsenal at the front and rear and around their hostages. The British were out to save their own skins and put the Gujaratis right at the back. Two of the wounded men were left where they lay and, only 4 miles along, the escapees abandoned the third by a small pond. The crew knew where they were heading – due east, five days' walk sounded perfectly feasible – but had no idea that this pond was the last water they would see on the journey.

Early on the first day's march the Tandroy closed in, armed men poised to attack. The king called out to one of his men to act as a negotiator and a bargain was struck. The crew would not be fired upon as long as the king was unharmed. That evening the king's wife was released and the crew settled down for the night, keeping a close watch on their two remaining hostages. King Kirindra must have been consumed with rage at the humiliation of being marched through his own country by these *vazaha mena*. The next day, shadowed by the Tandroy warriors, they walked until noon when the negotiator again came forward. He had a proposition for them – would they release the king in return for six guns? The captains had a tough decision. Weapons or hostages – which were going to be the better protection? Given that they still had the king's nephew, they chose the guns, and demanded a promise that the Tandroy would not follow them any further.

The king's release was met with shouting and gunfire from the jubilant soldiers and the crew were astounded to see Kirindra's sons paying the traditional respect of licking their father's feet. The party headed off and still the warriors followed them. At sunset the crew set up camp entirely surrounded by their pursuers. By morning they were so thirsty that they licked the dew from the grass.

During the following day – their third day labouring through an inhospitable landscape, guided only by the sun – they reached a low hill on top of which the Tandroy had placed a giant tub of rum. Sam suspected a ruse to intoxicate or poison the crew and pushed it over before anybody could give in to their overpowering thirst and drink from it. The negotiator came forward to suggest yet another bargain – the king's nephew should be swapped for 'three of the Head men of the Country'. Captain Young agreed, but on condition that the negotiator was one of them. The negotiator declined on the grounds that his family would be too distraught but offered his 'brother', without similar family commitments, in his place.

After releasing the prince in exchange for three fresh hostages, the crew realised they had made a terrible mistake. They could see the warriors coming ever closer and even marching in front of them. The new hostages were evidently expendable and the Tandroy war party was now at full strength and ready to spill blood. The killing began. One of the first to die was a crippled boy who couldn't keep up with his shipmates any longer. When the Tandroy came upon him, they pulled off his wooden leg and taunted him, before killing him with their spears. As night fell the crew listened to the urgent advice of their nervous hostages – after pretending to make camp, they all managed to slip away into the darkness in a final attempt to throw off their pursuers. At sunrise the party climbed a small hill and saw the Mandrare river, a long way off but, with luck, within reach.

They pressed on but elation turned to despair when, just a mile from the river, the Tandroy army caught up with them. Some of the exhausted sailors were straggling by now and the first to fall to the Tandroy spears were twenty or so men who were caught when they stopped to rest in the shade. Robert Drury, who had been marching near the back of the party, tore off his coat and ran as fast as he could. Hearing a musket shot, he turned to see the woman who had been walking beside him fall to the ground where she was promptly speared. They were now coming for him. He reached the river running, wading across and gulping water scooped up in his hat. Those of the crew who had already crossed the river formed up with their guns on the east bank, holding off the Tandroy advance, and Drury managed to reach the far side unharmed. When it was clear that no other stragglers were going to make it, the party headed onwards through a wood.

The Tandroy still came after them, picking off another three or four men as they stumbled through the trees. Two miles further and the wood petered out. The crew found themselves facing a limitless desert of sand. Impossible to shake off their pursuers in these parching dunes, impossible to hide in such a naked landscape; the only option was to stand and fight. Reaching a sandhill, the crew split up into four armed groups under each of the captains and John Benbow, the *Degrave*'s second mate, while the rest of them hid in a little gully.

The Tandroy dug themselves into the sand and began firing from different directions. With just thirty-six guns between them, the crew returned fire. Almost three hundred years later we walked across the sandhills east of the Mandrare, looking for any traces of this little battle. We knew that the shipwrecked sailors had soon run short of ammunition and were reduced to improvising with coins for musket balls. All their shot ran out as darkness was falling. In desperate straits they decided to send out Dudey the Malagasy woman and her husband to parley. Under a flag of truce – a little piece of red silk tied to the end of a spear – these two went to bargain for everyone's lives. The Tandroy agreed to spare the crew only if they surrendered their weapons there and then. Clinging to their last hopes of a deal, the men gave up their guns and, in return, the Tandroy told Dudey that they would let everyone go – but not until the next morning.

Yet the British were not quite as defeated in spirit as the Tandroy thought. Given the string of broken promises over the last few days, Captain Drummond and several others had concealed their guns rather than hand them over in the cease-fire. They had plans of their own for the following morning. As they huddled in the sand dunes that night, somewhere around 9 May 1703, the castaways, among them the fifteen-year-old Robert Drury, must have reflected on the string of unlikely events that had led to this predicament.

Death was haunting them. Disease and drowning had killed half the *Degrave*'s original crew before the ship even began the return leg of her voyage. Numbers had been topped up in Bengal and Mauritius and there were probably well over 130 people alive on that sandhill at dusk. Only three ever returned to Britain.

Thrown together briefly by the accidents of shipwreck and piracy, the fates of the small company of British sailors and the desperately unlucky Indian seamen were about to unravel. After night had fallen about thirty of the group crept off into the darkness, away from their shipmates and friends. This band included John Benbow and Robert Coleson – second mate and midshipman from the *Degrave* – as well as Drummond and Stewart, four of their men, and Dudey and her husband. They laboured across miles of sand dunes, around a lake and along the coast of Anosy, arriving safely in Fort Dauphin on the evening of 14 May 1703.

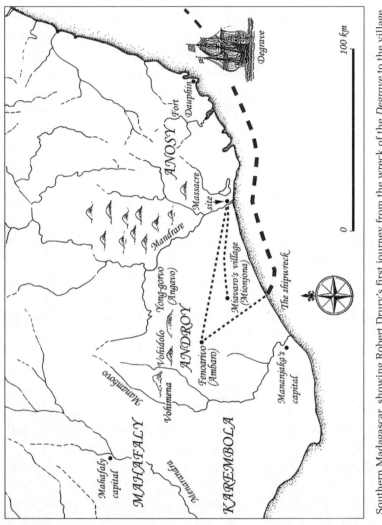

Southern Madagascar, showing Robert Drury's first journey from the wreck of the *Degrave* to the village where he spent eight years as a slave.

Here they were warmly received by Abraham Samuells, who promised them 'affection and friendship'. In the event, after four months of feeding and housing these unexpected guests, Samuells decided that they should raise their own food rather than continuing to be a burden on his resources. Benbow and eleven others then set off up the fever-ridden east coast to Matatana, where they stayed for a year, hoping for rescue. None came. Half of this party died there in Matatana and the rest decided to return to Fort Dauphin. It is nowhere recorded what happened to the Gujarati sailors or Dudey but perhaps she at least got home in the end.

However, it seems one of the British castaways stayed put on the east coast. Over two years later, towards the end of 1705, a Dutch slaver from the colony at the Cape of Good Hope called at Matatana. The *Ter Aa* took on board a hundred slaves and a lost Englishman. This was Robert Coleson, a junior midshipman from the *Degrave*, who had sloped off from the sandhill and made it safely to Fort Dauphin. His story from then is unclear, particularly as he may have tried to conceal time spent among the pirates, but Coleson had certainly reached Matatana somehow and survived there long enough for rescue to arrive. Coleson arrived at the Cape aboard the *Ter Aa* in January 1706 but there he vanishes. A statement of his story was sent to Amsterdam in March 1706 but the records do not say whether he ever went back to England.

By then news of the fate of the *Degrave* and of the Scottish ship the *Speedy Return* had already reached Britain. Other survivors had actually made it home. Two of Drummond's crew, Israel Phippany and Peter Freeland, had escaped from their pirate captors during a stop at Mauritius, whence they were rescued by the *Raper*, an English ship. When the *Raper* arrived in Portsmouth in March 1705, it also had on board a boy originally from the *Degrave*, picked up on St Helena where he had been deposited by another unknown ship.

The *Raper*'s purser posted a garbled account of the fate of the *Degrave*'s crew, muddled with the loss of the *Speedy Return*. The evidence of Phippany and Freeland, Drummond's two crewmen, concerning all that had happened to them – and who was responsible – was tragically ignored. In Scotland a story that the *Speedy Return* had fallen into the hands of murderers and pirates had already spread like wildfire. Rumour attributed the murders to the entirely innocent men of an English ship named the *Worcester*. In spite of the testimony of the returning crewmen from the *Speedy Return*, a mob in Leith lynched the captain and two men of the *Worcester* in April 1705.

The two Scotsmen and the boy from the *Degrave* carried home by the *Raper* brought the first news of the disaster, though the loss had already been assumed a certainty given that the *Degrave* was nearly two years overdue. She had not been seen or heard of since leaving Mauritius in February 1703. The story made the London papers although details were very muddled: 'That the Degrave, belonging to the New Company, coming homewards, was necessitated in great Distress to put for Madagascar; and that the Pyrates of that Island seiz'd her and murther'd all her Crew, a little Boy only excepted.'

We do not know the identity of this boy picked up from St Helena. He may have been one of the twenty-one midshipmen listed on the muster and some scholars interested in the fate of the *Degrave* have suggested that he was Robert Drury himself. Drury, though, would have been nearly eighteen in March 1705, hardly a 'little boy' in anyone's terms. Perhaps the boy had been a very young midshipman or cabin boy (there had certainly been a captain's boy on board), or even the child of one of the passengers.

In the following weeks stories abounded. In London the diarist Narcissus Luttrell entered in his journal for 21 April the news that the *Degrave* had sprung a leak and its crew had landed on Madagascar, carrying their guns on shore 'but could get no provision of the inhabitants, who said 'twas not customary to supply strangers till they delivered up their arms; which they had no sooner done, but those barbarous people killed them all but the boy now come over'.

Various versions of the news of the *Degrave*'s disaster spread back to the Indian Ocean. In May 1705 the Dutch at the Cape wrote that the *Degrave* had been abandoned and her crew taken prisoner by King Samuel the pirate. Two reports from India in late 1705 recorded the 'Degrave lost at Madagascar the ship Compa. killed Capt. Young & were afterwards killed by the Natives' and 'most, if not all, cut off by the natives'.

So Robert Coleson and the unknown boy had arrived back and told their stories. Another eye-witness was soon to appear. John Benbow, the son of Admiral Benbow, was alive and well in Fort Dauphin, waiting for rescue. After the abortive excursion to Matatana Benbow had gone back to Fort Dauphin with other survivors. Here they settled down to the basics of survival, growing sweet potatoes and other vegetables. Luckily for Benbow, Cape Dutch ships were regulars on the Madagascar slave routes – a quarter of all the slaves in the Cape colony in the 1700s were brought there from Madagascar. A year after rescuing Coleson from Matatana, the *Ter Aa* sailed into Fort Dauphin.

By this time Benbow, dressed as a Malagasy after more than three years in the country, was the only one left alive. No one knows exactly what happened to Captains Drummond and Stewart. When the *Ter Aa* arrived in Fort Dauphin late in 1706, they were no longer there. They had either died or had given up waiting for rescue from a friendly ship and departed with the pirates. Drummond is said to have wandered around Madagascar's ports for years, eventually meeting a nasty end at the hands of a Jamaican pirate named Lewis. John Benbow was all alone.

The Dutch ship left Madagascar on New Year's Eve 1706 with a cargo of slaves and took Benbow to the Cape colony. There he made a verbal deposition in which he described the whole nightmarish experience, dispatched in a letter from the Cape to Amsterdam in February 1707. By the time John Benbow came back to London, his father the admiral was dead. John wrote a lengthy account of his adventures in Madagascar which was read by his friends but the manuscript was soon lost, accidentally burnt in a house fire near Aldgate in 1714. Benbow himself did not last as long. He died on 22 November 1708, aged around twenty-seven, and was buried in St Nicholas's church-yard in Deptford.

With the return of Benbow to London, it must have seemed to the East India Company and to the families of the missing men that the story was over, the case closed. The various accounts circulating about the ship's fate were garbled but enough of the truth was known – the *Degrave* had sunk off southern Madagascar and the crew had been slaughtered by the inhabitants. Nothing more could ever emerge. Benbow knew that he had been the last Englishman left alive in Fort Dauphin and it was unlikely that, years after the event, any more castaways would be retrieved. Yet ten years later another survivor did appear, with a shocking tale to tell. That man was Robert Drury.

Robert Drury survived the massacre on the Mandrare river. He was not among Drummond and Benbow's party who escaped to Fort Dauphin – he stayed on the sandhill to the bitter end. Dawn brought the awful realisation to the hundred or so exhausted men remaining in the dunes that their companions had deserted them in the night. A Tandroy delegation approached the party and asked Sam the interpreter what had become of Captain Drummond and the others. Sam told them and all hell broke loose.

The *Degrave*'s captain Nicholas Young was the first to die, a Tandroy spear in his throat. In the orgy of killing only the youngest boys – Robert Drury and a handful of the other midshipmen – escaped death. Sam too was spared but all the others were slaughtered by the Tandroy.

The warriors robbed the corpses of their clothes, ripped open the bellies of several of the dead and then made haste to cross back over the River Mandrare into their own territory. As the war party began to march its young prisoners back into Androy, Drury could barely walk from hunger and thirst but staggered back past the mangled bodies of his dead companions. The Tandroy were now going their separate ways, small groups heading home in different directions. At noon the next day the party that had laid claim to Drury reached some trees and a pond – and Drury realised that he was back where he had started. Three days earlier the escapers had wandered through the woods within 200 yards of this precious water source – and their Tandroy hostages had said nothing.

That evening Drury's captors brought him to a village where 'we no sooner enter'd, but the Women and Children flock'd round about me, pinch'd me, struck me on the Back with their Fists, and shew'd several other Tokens of their Derision and Contempt; at which I could not forbear weeping'. Drury was lucky to be alive but what now faced him was a life of captivity and labour. He was to live nearly fourteen years in Madagascar, eight of them as a slave of the Tandroy.

6

The Land of Thorns

When we started exploring the story of Robert Drury, and the ship that brought him to Androy, there were several paths to follow. By delving into historical sources we were able to track down the pirates of Madagascar and a wealth of information about the world to which Drury belonged back in England. But how could we find out more about Drury's experiences in Madagascar in the early eighteenth century? There are no other written accounts that gave any details about life in Androy at that time. The only route open to us was the archaeology – to go there and try to find any surviving traces of the ancient history of the south.

Going to Androy would also take us down another path. In the book he wrote about his years in Madagascar Drury describes the lives and customs of the people with whom he lived, but what sort of world do the Tandroy live in today? The last three hundred years have seen significant changes to the planet and its inhabitants. Probably no one lives exactly as their ancestors did. Would we find that Tandroy society has changed beyond all recognition since Drury described it in the early 1700s? We set off to find out.

One August night we arrived by Landrover in a small village in northern Androy. The smiling faces of women and children appeared out of the darkness. There was laughter and shouting and many hands to shake. We were not the *vazaha* ('foreigners') whom they hoped we might be – Georges their French neighbour or Sarah the American – but we were clearly *vazaha mena*, 'red foreigners'. More importantly, Retsihisatse – whose village this was – was with us and he was not dead after all.

Three of us – Karen, Mike and the Malagasy archaeologist Ramilisonina – had headed south from Madagascar's capital Antananarivo almost a week before. Ramil had introduced Mike to the hazards of driving on the narrow winding roads of the highlands, with many warnings of how dangerous Malagasy roads could be. We had already worked that out for ourselves – the beer lorries hurtling past were missing us by a whisker. We spent the first night of our journey in Fianarantsoa, an attractive hill town at the southern limit of the highlands, and the next day we drove to the end of the 'good run' – the *goudron* or tarmac – and followed the dirt road into the grasslands of the Bara cattle pastoralists. We bumped ever southwards at a snail's pace along the rutted mud of the only road to Androy and after three dusty days reached the little town of Andalatanosy. Since there was nowhere to stay, we called on the town's Tandroy *président*, a Monsieur Clovis, who put us up in his rather nice concrete house.

The landscape of Androy was a tremendous contrast to the paddy-fields of the highland valleys and the wooded hills around Fianarantsoa. This was a parched and stony land, with scanty clumps of most peculiar trees and small fields with miserable-looking crops which we could not even identify. A surprising characteristic of the vegetation was the ubiquitous cactus, of the prickly pear or 'bunny ear' variety.

Cactus, known to the Tandroy as *raketa*, was first introduced to southern Madagascar around 1770 during an attempt by the French to re-establish their colony at Fort Dauphin, abandoned a century earlier. This new plant thrived and soon spread throughout the south. In Tandroy opinion *raketa* makes an ideal fencing material, being dangerously spiny, and is also a vital source of food and water. People gather the fruit and in the dry season cattle are fed on the juicy 'leaves', which are cut down with machetes and burnt to remove the spines.

Early accounts of Androy from the late 1800s and early 1900s describe a land so densely covered in cactus that it formed impenetrable forests, protecting villages so closely that they were almost invisible and quite inaccessible to passers-by. These prickly defences enabled the rebellious Tandroy to resist the colonial French authorities for many years after their arrival in 1900 and the colonisers dealt with the problem in one of the earliest incidents of biological warfare. They introduced the cactus-eating cochineal beetle from their island colony of Réunion. It reached Androy in 1928 and killed all the cactus; the Tandroy cattle died in their thousands of thirst and starvation. The ensuing famine lasted several years and resistance to colonial rule collapsed. Thereafter beetle-resistant strains of prickly pear were reintroduced and today it is again an essential part of life and landscape in Androy. We were to discover that almost everything in Androy is either prickly or poisonous and working among the cactus turned out to be hair-raising. The 2-inch-long spines are vicious enough to puncture tyres so can cause painful wounds, and when the *raketa* is in flower it sheds microscopic barbed hooks which embed themselves in the skin and eyes.

As we explored Andalatanosy that evening it was clear from the curious stares that tourists did not pass this way very often. Nobody looked well fed and the town water supply, pumped from deep underground, had run dry. Thunder rolled over the surrounding hills and a few miserable drops of rain fell on the desiccated soil. In the dark of Clovis's best bedroom Mike and Ramil talked about the possibility of picking up Robert Drury's 300-year-old trail, and how to find out how accurate his stories about Androy actually were.

We had first come to Madagascar two years before and visited the highlands and the east coast, somehow getting by with not a word of Malagasy, without even a phrase-book. Although the grammatical structure of Malagasy is said to be fairly simple, it is hard for a European visitor to get their head round a language which has, for example, no verb 'to be'. It is even harder to get one's tongue round the astonishingly long names of people and places. Pronunciation is usually fairly straightforward for an English speaker, with some anomalies too complicated to venture into here. As a rough rule of thumb for the reader, in long words the stress is on the penultimate syllable (as in the Man-am-*boo*-voo river, for example). The language was first written down by the French and, oddly, the Welsh, so the spelling does have some peculiarities.

We had a wonderful time on the east coast among the Betsimisaraka people where a kindly stranger took us to his family's ancestor ceremonies, although we never made it to the pirate island of Ile Sainte Marie. It turned out to be remarkably difficult to get on and off the island on Air Madagascar's overbooked little planes and we also discovered that the island's weather can be extremely wet – not quite the tropical paradise we had imagined.

We had interesting moments dealing with the quirky Malagasy cuisine. The amount of rice we consumed was, in our opinion, phenomenal but in our hosts' eyes, barely adequate. The Malagasy eat more rice than anyone else in the world and we could never keep up. In the capital we ate croissants from plates inscribed with the puzzling motto '*Nos ancêtres les Gaulois*' – the French had definitely left their mark. In the country we ate beef with the fur on – reading Drury's story should have forewarned us that the rural Malagasy don't skin their animals before cooking. After this first visit to the country, we came home knowing that we loathed manioc but really liked fried moths.

Back in Britain, we contacted Karen Middleton, an anthropologist who had just spent a year in the little coastal region of Karembola, Androy's western neighbour, and thought seriously for the first time about Robert Drury and the book he wrote. This work was published in 1729 under the title *Madagascar: or, Robert Drury's Journal, during Fifteen Years Captivity on that Island.* We learned that some literary critics thought this book to be a work of fiction, written not by Robert Drury at all but by Daniel Defoe, a tale of 'Robinson Crusoe meets the natives'. But unlike all other western academics who have puzzled over *Robert Drury's Journal*, Karen Middleton had worked in the arid south of Madagascar and knew the people. She had found that Drury's book contained details of life and language which could not have been invented and was utterly convinced that it was a true story. Someone in the eighteenth century had spent a long time in Androy.

We were particularly interested in the giant tombs that the Malagasy build for their dead even though they live in small and insubstantial houses. The Tandroy sounded fascinating. They construct the most impressive stone tombs, yet live in the flimsiest of wooden houses, which are burned to the ground after their occupant's death. We made plans for a research project to investigate the development of stone tomb-building in Androy. It wasn't the right moment to ask anyone for help to go looking for some long-dead English sailor but the tale gradually got its claws into us until Mike's colleagues were sick to death of his obsessive talk in the pub after work of pirates and shipwrecks.

Through John Mack, an Africa expert at the British Museum, we were able to get in touch with Madagascar's Musée d'Art et d'Archéologie. John and the Malagasy archaeologists came up with a crucial component of our fledgling project – transport. The Friends of the British Museum had raised funds for John to take a Landrover to Madagascar for a collecting trip in the 1980s and he had left it there for the use of the Malagasy museum. The 'Johnny Mack', as it is called, would be an indispensable means for our little team to get around in the south.

The project did not get off to an auspicious start. On a shoestring budget, our only choice of transport to Madagascar was by Aeroflot. Although the horror stories about that airline turned out to be grossly exaggerated, they did have a technical hitch of some sort and we got stuck in Moscow. At least we were able to start our research into monumental tombs by nipping out of the airport for a quick look at Lenin. We finally arrived in the capital Antananarivo bang in the middle of a general strike. There was nothing to do but sit in our hotel room and watch the crowds of demonstrators fill the capital's enormous market place each morning and afternoon. They apparently went home for lunch.

It was clear that the shortage of diesel caused by the strike was a major problem. We were going to be stuck for weeks so moved to a cheaper hotel, went to the market for some warm clothes and woolly socks to deal with the biting cold of the highland winter, and settled into a routine of study and analysis in the museum stores. There has been a considerable amount of archaeological research in Madagascar since the early 1960s and this was a golden opportunity to learn to recognise the types of ancient pottery found in Androy and to study the ethnographies that had been compiled by French and Malagasy anthropologists.

A month after arriving we left the capital with our Malagasy colleague Ramilisonina, with no idea how far we would get before our meagre fuel supply ran out. In Fianarantsoa we realised for the first time that Ramil is blessed with remarkable luck. Only one petrol station had any diesel at all and every car and lorry in town was parked in, at, on and around it. Ramil slipped on foot through the mayhem and persuaded an exasperated pump attendant to fill our jerry cans. We carried them away to the Landrover, tucked into a sidestreet away from the gridlocked traffic, and headed off into the south.

We were lucky to have made it as far as Andalatanosy – now we could start looking for traces of Robert Drury. That first morning Ramil asked our host Clovis the obvious question: did he know of a place called Fenoarivo, the name of the royal capital of King Kirindra? Clovis said yes, he *had* heard the name, but as the death-name of a prince whose tomb lay near the coast at the mouth of the Manambovo river. Malagasy attitudes to names are unlike our own. In the past the names of chiefs were always changed after death and the lists of ancient ancestors remembered by the Tandroy only record death-names until recent generations. Today names are still delicate things, not revealed to strangers. Children are not given their true name until they have survived infancy, being referred to as babies by endearments such as 'Cat's piss' and 'Puppy' to turn away misfortune.

So Clovis had given us a death-name – Andriampenoarivo. Like most such names, it began with *Andria*, meaning Chief or Prince, followed by a form of the word *fenoarivo*, which means 'full of a thousand' and has connotations of wealth and good fortune. Here was our first clue. A second lead came from the maps. Fenoarivo is a relatively common place-name in Madagascar yet it appears only once on the large-scale maps of Androy, at a spot marked in French as the '*mare de* (little lake of) Fenoarivo'. This lies only 20 miles from the sea, nothing like the 50 that Drury claimed he had walked from the shipwreck to King Kirindra's capital. It was worth investigating, however, so we headed off in the general direction of this pond. But first we needed to find someone who was Tandroy to join the team, since Ramil (whose family are Bezanozano, from the wooded eastern escarpment of the highlands) knew that here in the south he would be regarded as an outsider almost as much as we would.

He had last visited Androy eleven years before when he had worked with Retsihisatse, a Tandroy archaeologist and anthropologist who lived near Andalatanosy. We had to find him. Making a short stop in the next little town down the road, Ramil spotted Retsihisatse wheeling his bicycle across the road. After introductions and explanations – they had not met for years – Retsihisatse told us that yes, he would be very happy to be part of the project. He was willing to drop everything and leave with us immediately.

We celebrated our good fortune by having lunch in the one *hotely* (restaurant) in town. We had already been warned by Henry Wright, an American professor with years of experience in Madagascar, who had talked us through our plans, that this establishment served absolutely the worst food in the country – and he was right. As is usual for rural Madagascar the only item on the menu was meat stew and rice. The rice was full of small stones and even Retsihisatse, who lives here, thought the stew was awful. He pointed out the enormous size of the *hotely*'s overweight cat – it must be the only creature in town with the stomach to eat here.

Somewhat concerned about whether our guts would bear up but otherwise feeling that things were going well, the four of us set off, with Retsihisatse's bicycle on board, to the little lake which lay about 15 miles to the south. We explained ourselves to the local villagers and found someone who was happy to take us to the dried-up pond that they called Fanarive, the same place-name slightly altered. Here a *roandria* (noble or king) of the Tandroy named Bahary had once lived 'a long time ago'.

Archaeology involves a lot of fieldwalking – which is just what it sounds like. You walk systematically across fields, looking at the ground, concentrating hard. With practice you learn to recognise traces of ancient settlements, the most usual finds being pieces of broken pots. Fieldwalking around the dusty lake bed, we found a handful of pottery sherds and a single piece of nineteenth-century porcelain. If there had been a village here it had been insubstantial and short-lived and had not used much pottery. We were later to learn that Bahary died in about 1888, at a time when pottery was no longer being made although it was still in use.

The large-scale maps of Madagascar are usually fairly accurate and we soon noticed that the spot on the map marked as '*mare de Fenoarivo*' was not where we were standing. Perhaps we were in the wrong place. We spent the rest of the stifling hot day trudging through airless forests of spiny trees, following a baffled villager to lots of places that couldn't possibly be Fenoarivo pond and finding not a single piece of pottery anywhere.

We did not reach Retsihisatse's village until after dark. Retsihisatse had been expected home some ten hours earlier and there was consternation when the villagers heard the sound of an approaching car in the night. An unexpected vehicle could mean only the worst: he was dead and the police were bringing back his body. The surprise of our arrival was probably quite secondary to the relief felt by Retsihisatse's three wives who had seriously thought that they had lost their husband.

We decided to head for the coast to locate Clovis's tomb of 'Prince Fenoarivo' and do a round-trip of Androy to get a feel for the region and check on the possibilities of finding diesel. After that we would concentrate on a survey area in the rocky region of northern Androy, about 50 miles from the sea. In the dissected and eroding landscape of the hills we were likely to find traces of ancient settlements. It was also an area with hundreds of stone tombs which we could record from a respectful distance, to build up an idea of tomb styles and how they had changed in the last hundred years.

7

The People of the Tombs

Madagascar has lurid soil. It is often called the red island, and from the air the traveller sees vast pink fans of mud leaking from the river mouths into the Mozambique Channel and the Indian Ocean. In the highlands erosion scars carve red gashes in the treeless hillsides. For the British visitor, the elegant balconied houses of the highland Merina people have a certain familiarity as they are built in neat red brick.

We passed many smart but small Tandroy houses built out of red clay. Most country people in the south still live in tiny wooden houses of the type described by Robert Drury but in this northern part of Androy, where there is clay soil, the fashion for building in hand-made mudbrick has recently become very popular. Ramilisonina was intrigued by other changes since his last visit to Androy. The loincloth once worn by all men has largely disappeared and everybody now wears western clothing, topped off with Madagascar's ubiquitous *lamba*, a piece of material wrapped over the top of one's garments – the word translates into English as cloth, clothing or shawl. For Tandroy men the *lamba*, usually a blanket of pastel checks, is a multipurpose cloak. Foreigners' preconceptions about what they expect non-western people to look like can take quite a beating when it comes to fashion, which is truly global. Rural Madagascar has no television and rarely sees a magazine or newspaper yet in the early 1970s, for example, Tandroy girls wore miniskirts and young men coveted enormously flared trousers. This combination of global influences and local cultural habits creates a distinctive Tandroy style.

Men still carry spears but they are equally likely to be wearing a denim jacket beneath their *lamba*. Male youth culture expresses itself in the black trilby hat and plastic combs parked in the hair at jaunty angles. Preferences for particular colours among different groups are still evident – the Bara who live to the north of the Tandroy have a great predilection for blue – but Tandroy women today wear a wide range of colours. Women and girls never wear shorts or trousers; a skirt or dress is protected by a printed polyester *lamba* wrapped around the waist, reaching to below the knee. In recent years the most popular *lamba* are printed with images of the beautiful heroine of a wildly romantic Mexican soap opera which entranced Malagasy television audiences.

Everyone turns out in their best clothes for funerals, when hundreds of people gather to bury the dead in massive tombs. Near the little town of Jafaro we stopped – at a discreet distance – to look at a fine group of tombs. Their rectangular walls had standing stones at the east and west ends, indicating that these were the tombs of men as opposed to women. For the Tandroy, roadsides are perfect places to bury their dead. Tombs can be colossal, often over 20m long, and the traveller walking to the weekly market cannot fail to be impressed by the size and beauty of these monuments. The dead remain forever in the memory of the living who pass by.

The basic design of twentieth-century tombs consists of a heap of loose rubble enclosed by shoulder-high walls although the walls are constructed in various styles – dry-stone, mortared blocks or bare concrete. Tombs of the 1960s onwards are often adorned with paintings – of everything from cattle to aeroplanes and Elvis Presley – and with little house-like concrete structures constructed on top of the rock-filled interior. Earlier tombs, especially in the west, are sometimes ornamented with carved wooden posts. Cattle have always been sacrificed at Tandroy funerals and the bucrania (the upper part of the skull with horns attached) placed on the tomb. These only survive for about thirty years although the bottles and enamel bowls which are also left on the tomb survive for longer.

Although we had a lot to learn about the chronology of tomb styles, we knew that in Drury's day, the early eighteenth century, stone tombs did not exist. Then the dead were buried deep in the forests, in secret cemeteries that are still used today. Burial in the woods is often a sign that the family is not wealthy – to hold an elaborate funeral and build a highly visible stone tomb costs a great deal of money and not everyone can attain this desired ideal. Babies and very small children are also buried without great ceremony in graves in forest cemeteries.

With the advent of the bullock cart in the last sixty years, people living in the sandy parts of Androy can now import stone from many miles away in order to build a tomb. Stone quarries in the west of Androy specialise in producing tall, thin 'man stones', the standing stones which embellish the front and back walls of tombs. One also sees isolated standing stones, each adorned with a cattle skull perched on a thin wooden post. These are cenotaphs, memorials to men who died away from home and whose bodies were never returned to their ancestral lands for burial.

Stone is reserved for the ancestors. It is hard, it endures, it is permanent. Wood, soft and perishable, is for the living. This distinction is so marked that the wooden house inhabited for the short human lifespan is burnt to the ground once the deceased has departed to spend eternity in their stone tomb.

Although often highly visible, like the roadside monuments we saw that day outside Jafaro, Tandroy tombs must not be approached closer than, say, 10 or 20 metres. They have an invisible forcefield of sacredness around them which is only 'switched off' when people come to bury the dead or, more rarely, to clean the tomb. At every such occasion the blood of cattle must be spilt in a sacrifice to the ancestors. The area around a tomb cannot be cultivated or used for collecting wood. It belongs to the ancestors and not to the living.

Beyond the roadside tombs outside Jafaro, the fine dirt road stopped abruptly. It was built for the convenience of a ministerial delegation to a prominent politician's home village and continued no further. The rough track became narrower and, like fingernails on a blackboard, the thorny trees that line the way were soon scratching the paint off the Landrover's sides. In the middle of nowhere we chanced upon a tiny hamlet, just two houses in a clearing in the wood. Men came out to warn us away – they were in the middle of a curing ceremony for a sick child and we must not interrupt. Deeper into the forest we stopped in another clearing and found definite signs of an abandoned village. From the look of the pottery sherds we picked up, there had been a settlement here in the nineteenth century. All that remained were scattered pieces of broken pot and some fragments of animal bone; a few small upright stones had once supported cooking pots on household hearths.

Tandroy villages do not stay still. They expand as children grow up and marry – the young couple's new house is built south of the parents' home. They contract as people die or migrate in search of work and adventure. Since houses are destroyed at death, there is an inherent impermanence in any settlement and only the tombs are built with any thought of durability. Life is transitory – only death and the clan are eternal. If misfortune plagues a village, the entire community will up and move. Some villages marked on maps as little hamlets turn out to be densely populated and cover vast areas; others have vanished altogether since the villagers have moved away, leaving few traces behind them.

During our field surveys we were often taken to sites of abandoned nineteenth-century villages. People know the whereabouts of the settlements inhabited by their immediate predecessors and can also tell their ancient history, in terms of the routes followed by their distant ancestors during their journey from the east to settle in Androy. Our problem as archaeologists was to find the places settled during the course of those long-ago migrations, ancient villages whose exact positions are usually long forgotten.

There is a distinct difference between towns and villages. Embedded in the ramshackle town architecture is another history – the brief period of colonisation by the French. The highland kingdom of Imerina, which effectively ruled Madagascar in the nineteenth century, had contact with the British and then the French from 1816. Initially a meeting of equals, discussing treaties and trade, the encounter between the Merina and the French ended in invasion and colonisation by the European power in 1894. The Merina royal dynasty clung on but was eventually overwhelmed, and the last queen died in exile in Algeria in 1917.

The French subjugation of the distant south was more hotly contested. A bloody campaign involving Senegalese soldiers quelled the unruly Tandroy between 1900 and 1904 but the French were gone by 1960. In towns such as Tsiombe, which we reached that afternoon, their traces remain in decaying and deserted stone buildings. Tsiombe, on the west bank of the Manambovo river, was built by the French as an administrative post on the only road running east–west across the far south of Madagascar. Today the town's residents prefer to live in small wooden houses which fill the spaces between the dilapidated colonial buildings.

To cross the Manambovo by car one must go to Tsiombe. The bridge always has a few holes but is usually driveable. This bridge seemed slightly superfluous at the season when we first saw it. The Manambovo is one of the three major watercourses of the south but for many months of the year it is completely dry: the riverbed of yellow sand winds towards the sea through steep cliffs gouged out by the floodwaters of the rainy season. This riverbed is pockmarked with crater-like holes where women patiently scoop out tiny amounts of grey water into calabashes. In later weeks we learned to appreciate such riverbed water-holes: the underground water is clean if a little sandy. Elsewhere our water sources were inhabited by a variety of creatures great and small – from herds of cattle, through the usual pond life, to the troublesome microbes which afflicted all of us from time to time.

At a little *hotely* in Tsiombe's market square we stopped for another meal of meat stew and rice and were soon surrounded

by gaping hordes of small boys. We squirmed with embarrass-
ment but had already realised that as naïve foreigners at large
in a strange land we could have done much worse.

The Malagasy are in general enormously polite in dealings
with one another and with strangers. The highland people
perceive the Tandroy as rather less well-mannered than they
might be – a little pushy and bold for Merina tastes, since the
southerners are known to be plain-speaking if not blunt, a
reputation comparable to that enjoyed by Yorkshiremen in
Britain. Anyway, baffled stares, rather than aggression or
contempt, were not too much to bear. Our language skills had
come on apace (we were now fluent in three words: 'rice',
'water' and 'hello') – so Mike tried a few tentative greetings to
the more harmless-looking children and was rewarded with
gales of laughter and a sudden increase in his audience. As
well as looking peculiar, we did tricks: everything we did was
comical or strange. We also had our first encounter with
Tandroy stoicism (or heartlessness) when dealing with injury
and illness. One young man in the crowd had horrible burns,
from drunkenly rolling into a fire. Charred flesh was falling
off his legs. He should have been whimpering with pain, but
he wasn't. He should also have been in hospital, but there
isn't one.

That evening, as night fell, Ramil and Retsihisatse peered
into the darkness along the road, looking for any sign of life –
the flickering light of a fire would eventually reveal a village.
The Malagasy seem to hate the idea of camping in the wild. In
all our years of fieldwork in Androy, no matter how late or
how lost we have been, our colleagues have never once agreed
to our pleas to just stop anywhere and wait till morning. They
will find a village, come what may.

Tandroy villagers' hospitality is hard to credit. To our
European eyes their kindness to strangers is most unexpected,
although perfectly natural to our Malagasy colleagues. That
night, in spite of the shock of the unforeseen arrival of some
very strange visitors, the village we descended on all got out of
bed and sorted out for us two empty houses in which to sleep,

even though in the darkness they could barely make out who or what we might be.

Tandroy houses are no bigger than they were in Drury's day, usually being less than 12ft long by 10ft wide – about the size of an English garden shed. The door is at the north end and traditionally the fireplace is directly inside, though many people have a small detached kitchen house. Older houses have two doors at the north end, one for guests and the other for the head of the household, and a third door on the west side, formerly used only by women and slaves. The doorways are tiny, often so low that one can only enter crouched double, sliding one's shoulders sideways through the narrow gap. There are no windows and no furniture. Everybody eats and sleeps on the earth floor, which is covered by rush mats woven in geometric patterns. Belongings are stored in the roof beams and, these days, in padlocked suitcases.

Everybody also locks their doors when they go out, which we find odd since there appears to be little danger from burglars in a village where everybody is related. Nevertheless, the flimsy wooden doors are always carefully locked up when the women go to the fields or to market. Since a woman's house actually belongs to her, and not to her husband, we have occasionally been received in villages by disconsolate men who have absolutely nowhere to go. They are locked out until the wife gets home because men don't have a key to their own house.

The next morning we arrived on the coast at Faux Cap (the 'false cape'), almost but not quite the southernmost point of Madagascar. A strong inshore wind lifted spray high into the air from the breakers just offshore. Here we walked among the dunes, through valleys and mountains of sand, looking for remains of any ancient fishing communities who may have once lived along the seashore. We discovered traces of two, as well as something for which we were unprepared. Huge spreads of broken eggshells carpeted some of the dunes. These were no ordinary shells but the remains of the eggs of giant flightless birds, now extinct, known as Elephant Birds or

Aepyornis maximus. Other than some recently discovered fossils from the Cretaceous period, these were the largest birds ever to have walked the earth.

At 11ft in height, Elephant Birds were not quite as tall as the New Zealand moa, hunted to extinction by the nineteenth century by the Maori, but they were bigger and heavier. Their eggs were larger than ostrich eggs and the pieces of eggshell which litter the coastal dunes are sometimes as thick as a china tea-cup. Very occasionally someone finds a complete unbroken egg which they can sell for a lot of money. Some people try to make a living by gluing broken shells back together, shaping fragments to fit where pieces are missing. In one of those Catch-22 situations, tourists can of course buy these eggs but, as with tortoiseshell and other natural resources, to export them from Madagascar is illegal.

Heading back inland, once again we left it very late to find a place to stay and were driving around in pitch darkness when we saw electric lights in the distance. We had thought that we were a long way from such technological wonders – even Tsiombe does not have electric lighting – so what was this? The map showed no villages, only a forest crossed by tracks made by bullock carts. The source of the mysterious lights turned out to be a mica mine, where the thin sheets of this flaky, translucent mineral were dug out from deep underground. The manager, a geologist from the highlands, was happy to put us up for the night and pleased to meet others with an interest in things subterranean. Not only could he provide us with shelter and water but he also had a supply of something that we had not seen for a week – he had storage tanks full of diesel and was happy to sell us some.

We spent the night on the concrete floor of one of the outbuildings, marvelling at the size of the cockroaches that roamed around and over us. Cockroaches are perfectly harmless but very smelly and taint food if they walk on it. In Britain, where they are almost unheard of, people see them only rarely, and our first close-up view of a cockroach of the Malagasy variety had been just a few days earlier. Back in

Retsihisatse's village we had inspected one which had set up home in the display panel of his transistor radio. We had thought that creature, a couple of inches long, was pretty big, but those sharing our beds at the mica mine were enormous. We found out why when we discovered their home base and restaurant: the cesspit beneath the privy holes.

This is probably one of the many reasons why the Tandroy don't dig latrines – why encourage nests of cockroaches? Tandroy attitudes to the body and its various functions are actually a lot more complicated than that. Certain activities, such as sleeping and eating, always take place indoors while others always happen outside. Every village has a communal open-air lavatory area, always to the west of the houses, away from the sacred east. Finding one's way in a strange village is no more complicated than being a visitor in a house back home, although the usual directions of 'upstairs, first on the left' become something like 'off west, over the stile and behind the big cactus'. You always know when you've reached the right spot. Discarded corn cobs and pecking hens take the place of our toilet paper and flushing water so a brief visit to the cactus can, unfortunately, put you right off chicken stew.

Leaving the mica mine and its scuttling wildlife the next morning, we visited an elderly descendant of the kings of the Tandroy. The old man told us that he and his ancestors belonged to the southern branch of the royal clan. His forebears had once lived at a place called Ampotake on the west bank of the Manambovo river. Buried near Ampotake was a *roandria* (chief or king) whose death-name was Fenoarivo.

Back across the Manambovo, villagers took us into the woods to show us the places that they associated with the ancient Tandroy kings. The man whose death-name was Prince Fenoarivo lies buried in a forest but this was a place of taboo which we could not enter: the sacredness of royal tombs and forests must never be violated. On the edge of the forest we found pottery of the late seventeenth century. This place was inhabited at the time of the greatest of the Tandroy monarchs – in the late 1600s sibling rivalry drove King Andrianjoma

northwards out of Ampotake, leaving his brother behind in the
south and forever splitting the royal dynasty into two branches.

Drury only saw the Manambovo river a couple of times
during his life in Androy and it was many days' walk from the
royal capital he knew. This settlement could not have been the
village of King Kirindra – it was possibly the right date but it
was in completely the wrong place. We were drawing a blank
on Fenoarivo but had arrived at a good time to learn more
about Tandroy life. During a night-time ceremony, accompanied by the rhythmic sounds of the *lokanga*, a three-stringed
violin, several villagers became possessed by spirits.

Tandroy boys sometimes improvise on home-made guitars
but we have seen the *lokanga* only very rarely. The other
Tandroy musical instrument, the *marovany*, is a long
rectangular sounding-box, strung on each vertical side, and is
also used in spirit possession ceremonies. The *marovany*
players are always men although there is often a female
accompanist shaking dried beans in tins.

Retsihisatse recorded the *lokanga* player at Ampotake on his
Walkman and on listening to the tape weeks later, we all
noticed that the sound of the instrument was almost drowned
by the breathy panting with which the musician accompanies
his playing. Westerners would probably find the same problem
with traditional performances of *marovany* music: the
hypnotic rattling of the maracas is an integral part of the event
and almost swamps the delicate melody of the instrument.
Some recordings of Tandroy *marovany* players have been
made very recently and tourists in the south can find them in
the Fort Dauphin hotels. Other instruments and styles of
singing from the east and west coasts turn up in the music
now available in Europe and visitors to the highlands will
certainly see the *valiha*, a tubular stringed instrument, and
hear accordion players – musicologists can identify old French
country tunes in the Malagasy accordion repertoire.

In later years we heard other types of Tandroy music. On
starry nights girls beat drums and sing to urge their suitors to
come and wrestle before them in the moonlight. Professional

praise-singers are paid to attend funerals and extemporise verses about the deceased and their families, an exhausting activity since they are expected to continue for hours on end over several days. Hymns both Protestant and Catholic are popular elsewhere in Madagascar – the highlands have been devoutly Christian for over a hundred years – and we have occasionally added a tentative English descant to the Malagasy hymns which are sung to the tunes of 'When the Saints Go Marching in' and, strangely, 'Auld Lang Syne'.

We lay in our tents in Ampotake with the noise of spirit possession going on into the small hours and emerged blearily at dawn into a dull, grey morning. It was cold, we were miserable and the dew-covered landscape looked disappointingly like Scotland. From the fog emerged a group of muffled figures, men wrapped tightly in their *lamba* against the damp. People were gathering here from distant villages to work on one of the nearby tombs. On the day of a Tandroy funeral, the coffin made from a hollowed-out tree-trunk is placed in a shallow grave less than a foot deep and then buried under an oval cairn of stones. In later months and years, when time, money and the omens permit, walls of stone and mortar are constructed around the cairn. Here at Ampotake the tomb under construction was that of a man who had died three years earlier. No one expected the work to be finished for at least another year.

That morning the extended family had gathered to collect rocks from a small quarry, carting them to the tomb to throw on top of the cairn within the tomb's walls. The tomb enclosure, which is always rectangular but can be any size – the bigger the better in Tandroy eyes – must be filled in with loose stones, burying the original cairn under layers of rubble which come up to the top of the shoulder-high walls. This was a great chance to find out more about tomb building and we asked if we might join in. Our offer was accepted with some amusement. As in most countries once colonised by the West, local-born and expatriate Europeans can be found in many towns in Madagascar in a variety of trades and professions, but to see white people doing manual work is a novelty to any Malagasy. Tandroy contact with foreigners is usually limited to missionaries and occasional aid workers and Mike's propensity for rock-heaving was possibly a bit of a surprise.

By noon the day's shift was over and the work party adjourned for lunch – the killing and cooking of a billy-goat. The main joints of meat were shared out raw for the various families to take home with them and the men ate a communal meal of *pitsoke*, blood and fat fried together, which is one of the prized dishes of Androy. The goat's sliced intestine (which looks and feels like calamari) also went in the pot, along with the entire contents of the stomach and guts, in various states of digestion ranging from fresh grass to incipient dung. Ramil tucked in with enthusiasm, but Mike made his apologies and withdrew.

8

The Hill of Ghosts

It was time to concentrate on tackling the landscape as archaeologists, leaving Drury's story until we were more sure of our ground. At that time only a handful of people believed that Robert Drury had ever been to Androy. Most academics interested in his book were convinced it had been written by Daniel Defoe. Were we looking for imaginary places described by a fictional character? We were in danger of going round in circles and might spend weeks looking for a site that would never be found, so we decided to head for an area further north, where the open vegetation would provide ideal conditions for fieldwalking to find ancient settlements. Retsihisatse was in favour because it would base us not too far from his home, in touch with people who would know who he was and where he was from.

That evening we almost wrecked the Landrover climbing up a boulder-strewn track to a small village to stay the night, but alongside the rocky 'road' we were pleased to find a lead musketball on a nineteenth-century settlement site. When we arrived at the hamlet on the crest of the hill, nobody was pleased about anything. The headman was away at market and one of the old women had to nag her sickly looking son into being welcoming. We were embarrassed at our imposition as this village was plainly very poor indeed.

Hospitality requires two things. Like it or not, the host must offer food and the guest absolutely has to eat at least some of it. Here there was nothing at all to eat except a pot of manioc boiled in a stew of bitter leaves. Manioc, a long red-skinned tuber, is the staple diet of all Tandroy, and it lives up to its name of *balahazo* (bullet-wood), having to be soaked and boiled for hours before you can get your teeth into it. When you finally manage to chew a lump or two, it tastes like a cross between raw potato and rotten wood.

In the morning we received the customary present of a chicken and reciprocated with a large gift of money because the villagers could clearly do with it. We would have to stay elsewhere. We needed to find a village that could stand having us around, possibly for weeks on end. We set off to have a good look at the terrain, thinking about how best to locate any ancient settlements. The first move was to find the highest hill and go up it to get a view of the area.

According to all sources to hand – the map, the locals and the look of the land – the crest we wanted to head for was Vohidolo, the 'hill of ghosts'. Nobody locally volunteered any suggestions as to how it had acquired that name but when we reached the top we had a pretty good idea why. At the summit a large flat area, encircled by stretches of very old dry-stone walling, was littered with broken pottery of styles used centuries before Drury's arrival in Androy in 1703. This was evidence of an earlier civilisation which had surrounded its settlements with stone walls rather than relying on the natural protection of the forests, as recorded by Drury in the early 1700s. Who had been here before the Tandroy? We might not find eighteenth-century Fenoarivo but here were remains of a much earlier phase in Androy's past.

The little towns of Madagascar have weekly markets and that afternoon we went shopping. All markets follow the same basic layout. Meat is sold in one area and vegetables and beans in another, displayed on mats on the ground and measured out by the *kapoake*, a standard measure which can only be translated as 'the quantity which can be heaped up in an empty condensed-milk tin', since this is the device used by traders everywhere. *Lamba* – crisp and gaudy before the sun fades them in use – hang like flags from clothing stalls and hardware such as spears also has its own corner.

Shopping requires huge reserves of time and patience. Our colleagues like to take it slowly, examining everyone's wares, searching out the best bargains and negotiating a little 'present' of a bit extra on each large purchase. We leave to Ramil and Retsihisatse the negotiations in the market; they prefer to do the serious shopping without us at their shoulders since prices naturally increase when the gullible 'red foreigners' come into view.

Water in Androy is precious. Washing is kept to an absolute minimum and everyone makes full use of chance supplies of water – pools in a tarmac road after a rainstorm attract crowds of people seizing the chance for a good wash. Being so hard to attain, cleanliness is a highly desirable state (soap is a popular present) and before arriving in town on market day, everyone stops at any nearby puddles to wash the dust from their faces and feet. And everyone wears their best clothes – they may make no sales and no purchases but they will be seen by their friends and neighbours. After walking for hours through dusty, prickly scrub in soaring temperatures, market-goers manage to arrive in town looking impressively crisp and clean. Except for us.

We had got so used to being grubby that we somehow failed to notice the transformations from ragged old clothes to pristine elegance that were going on around us. The pointing and staring as we walked through the market's colourful bustle was more than just surprise at seeing foreigners – it was amazement that anybody would come to town so dirty and underdressed. It was an embarrassing moment, like turning up at a wedding in one's gardening clothes.

Retsihisatse, who had gently tried to persuade us to wash our filthy feet in a convenient ditch that morning, surely despaired of our many *faux pas* in that first year's work. Living with the two of us must have been like being saddled with a pair of obstinate and faintly stupid small children. We were ignorant and demanding, yet incapable of saying what we wanted. Our linguistic skills were not exactly increasing by leaps and bounds – it took us a week just to learn to say his name properly. Our vocabulary had doubled and we now knew the word for 'bucket' and two adjectives, 'hot' and 'blue'. We could chat with Retsihisatse about only two subjects, either the weather (definitely hot) or our new blue bucket. He was very patient.

That evening we searched for somewhere to stay for the next three weeks and luck was on our side when we happened upon a small village full of smiling and confident people, happy to take us in. Better still, they had a new UNICEF-installed water pump which tapped the deep artesian flow far below the ground's parched surface. Best of all, they knew of strange stone ruins nearby.

These turned out to be ancient tombs, which whetted our appetite for our main task, to find out about the origins of the Tandroy's impressive burial monuments, but that afternoon our tomb project developed a hitch. Although we could go fieldwalking wherever we wanted, the lunar month of August to September was starting and this was a particularly inauspicious time of the year when subjects concerning death and tombs should not be raised. None of the anthropologists we had consulted had ever mentioned this little point. Our plans to ask a lot of questions about funerals and tomb building were clearly scuppered.

Everywhere else in Madagascar this is the time each year when the dead are honoured and even brought out of their tombs for their bony remains to be danced among the living in noisy celebrations involving hundreds of people. As we were to find out again and again, the Tandroy do like to do things differently. Not only are they a 'contrary culture', but their multitude of taboos often seem designed deliberately to make life hard for themselves.

To add to our gloom Ramil was leaving us. He was needed on a field project in the north and would have to fly from Fort Dauphin that weekend. All this time we had communicated with Retsihisatse through Ramil. How were we going to manage when no one else spoke any French? And what were we going to do without Ramil to be lucky for us? Moreover, there were no choices left about fieldwork sites. There was barely enough diesel remaining to get us back to the capital at the end of the survey so the Landrover was going to have to stay put except for occasional trips to market. We were going to be on foot, on our own.

The next day we made a final journey, which led us to paradise, also known as Fort Dauphin. We were there by lunchtime, crossing with startling speed from barren desert and spiny forest to the lush tropical forests of the east coast. Fort Dauphin is beautiful, abundant in fruit and fish, and there is always beer – ice cold at that. As we lay beneath the palm trees on the sands of Libanona beach and looked out across a blue sea worthy of a holiday brochure, we pondered on the twists of fate. This heavenly place was the region chosen by the Musée's chief archaeologist as his study area whereas we were slogging around in what appeared to be the setting for *Mad Max II*. Ramil maintained stoutly that it was a matter of ethnic personality and character. The Tanosy of the south-east are said to be rather stand-offish and unwelcoming and we were very lucky to be working with the forthright Tandroy whose resilience and independence Ramil had greatly admired the first time he came to the region. And besides, because there is no water in Androy, there are no mosquitoes.

The little airfield outside Fort Dauphin was swarming with tourists stranded by the month-long general strike. There had been no flights for days but Ramil, who can charm the birds from the trees, got the last seat on the first plane out that week. With apprehensive hearts we waved him off. As soon as he had gone Retsihisatse promptly revealed that he *could* speak French and really quite well. We discovered we understood a lot more Malagasy than we had hitherto realised. It was going to be fine.

Back in the village, the following weeks took on a steady routine. Everyone was up at the crack of dawn, fetching water and lighting fires. Retsihisatse relished cooking the breakfast of salty *kitoza*, ropes of sun-dried beef toasted in the fire's ashes. After a morning's fieldwalking he would edge us homewards at noon, towards the village and a steaming pot of rice. The Tandroy dislike picnics – meals should be hot and eaten indoors whenever possible – and it was only in later years that we learnt how to persuade everyone to eat a packed lunch in the fields occasionally.

At the end of the day's work we would return at dusk and sit watching the brief tropical sunset, drinking home-made rum. *Toakagasy*, illicitly distilled rum, is made everywhere in Madagascar. Although technically illegal until recently, it is so much a part of life that the national radio's round-up of consumer prices and inflation has always included *toakagasy* as a staple commodity. The village where we had settled had an ample supply. Hidden deep in the woods was a heap of sugar cane and a large oil-drum still which produced an extremely palatable clear spirit. Sometimes it can be fearful stuff but we were fortunately in a village of experts. Buying their product had beneficial effects all round. Without being patronisingly philanthropic, we were moving money into the villagers' pockets, and Mike and Retsihisatse slept like babies.

Supper was another huge mound of rice, after which site records and diaries were written up. Most of our candles had melted in the heat and there was no paraffin to light a lamp so we were normally in bed by eight o'clock. Although a visitor to a Tandroy village will often sleep with the host family, Retsihisatse spent every night in the Landrover. The man of the house was away and we were there for a long time, so good manners prevented him from staying in the family home. He is a broad-shouldered man, over 6ft tall, and finally admitted at the end of our fieldwork that after weeks in the Landrover his back was killing him – but in that first year he never accepted our offer of a tent.

We slept in a little house, about 6ft wide by 8ft long, where we also ate our meals and worked. Fortunately it was only towards the end of our stay that Karen found out who lived in the fist-sized cocoons on its walls. We were sharing with the biggest spiders we had ever seen – the sort that ought to be behind glass in a zoo – and Karen was terrified. Some spiders in Androy are extremely poisonous, not that anyone ever takes any notice of them. Strangely the Tandroy are generally very scared of snakes even though none of those in Madagascar is dangerous. We all have our phobias and a subsequent field season even revealed Mike's secret fears. We had never expected to meet frogs in the dry country of Androy but they do exist, and after heavy rain hibernating frogs and turtles burrow up from deep underground. A clammy intruder hopping on to his lap one damp night sent Mike and his dinner flying.

Madame president, our hostess, was a warm-hearted woman who found the activities of her foreign guests a source of great amusement. Working in the fields with her neighbours one day, she spotted Mike striding along in a determined fashion and, to gales of laughter, imitated his walk. The Tandroy shuffle is a very distinctive gait, walking with feet splayed outwards in a casual stroll born of traversing soft sand. Foreigners not only didn't walk like normal people, they even had trouble sitting down properly. We both found our legs were not bendy enough to squat for long periods and we got the occasional ticking-off for bad table-manners – our feet and bottoms were always in the wrong place or at the wrong elevation at dinnertime.

Retsihisatse and one of the young men of the village hit it off immediately and soon discovered that they had an ex-wife in common. The Tandroy are polygamous, and divorce and remarriage are very common. Men like to have more than one wife, a sign of wealth and status. There is no maximum permitted number but it is extremely expensive to support several households, so many men only have one wife at a time and more than three is rare.

The causes of marital breakdown are probably the same as anywhere – private lives are private the world over. Adultery certainly happens and is punished by the guilty man paying a fine in cattle. Interestingly, there has been little inflation in three hundred years – the number of cattle to be paid remains the same as it was in Drury's day. In Androy divorce is controlled by the husband. A woman can manoeuvre a divorce by perpetually going home to her father until the deserted husband finally gives up the struggle but he always has the right to refuse his wife a divorce. Men may instigate divorce but they also bear the consequences. They are obliged to feed and house an ex-wife until she marries again (and she may choose not to) and must take on responsibility for their children. The children of divorced parents always stay with their father, so many Tandroy grow up being cared for by stepmothers. Babies do remain with divorced mothers but at about the age of three a child must be sent back to its father. Outright neglect is rare – a bad stepmother will be unpopular and contact is always maintained with the mother's family.

Tandroy girls know that they will live their adult lives in a succession of different villages, moving house each time they remarry, sometimes travelling great distances to live and work with new neighbours and co-wives. As well as hoping for babies of their own, they can expect to look after other women's children at some point in their marital career. For Tandroy boys, unless they leave as young men to see the world and earn some money, home is home. They live their lives in one place, alongside their father, uncles and brothers.

The young man with whom Retsihisatse had struck up a friendship fieldwalked with us occasionally but we spent most days in the company of the youngest son of our host, a boy of about ten, who took to archaeology with great enthusiasm. Although disabled by a withered leg, he got about with a stick and never missed a chance to explore the stony hills and valleys around his village. There were odd moments of drama. One morning we were surveying in a small valley inhabited by a *kokolampo*, a spirit of the rocks and trees, when our unexpected appearance startled three small girls collecting water. They dropped their buckets and ran away screaming. A little while later their father – armed to the teeth with spear, axe and sling – and grandmother arrived. All Tandroy know tales of strangers who steal children's hearts and livers and these adults had come out prepared to face monsters. Fortunately the elderly woman recognised us from our stay in her village several weeks before and the situation was defused. Yet it taught us something we would come up against time and time again. Children, young women and even adult men can be extremely frightened by the sight of a *vazaha mena* (red foreigner) but the old ladies fear nothing.

The results of our archaeological survey were very exciting and we recorded more stone-walled ruins, four in all. This was not South America so they were not exactly lost cities but they had once been substantial constructions, occupied a thousand to five hundred years ago. As every archaeological television documentary likes to ignore, if structures are visible above the ground then there is really no such thing as a 'lost' site. Here, as elsewhere in the world, the locals already knew about the existence of the ruins even if the foreign archaeologists didn't.

Although the villagers did not know what the stone ruins were, and certainly had no dates for them, they called them *manda*, a word from the Swahili language spoken on the East African coast. One of these *manda* had been an important place: the fineness of the masses of broken pottery and the quantities of cattle bones indicated that great feasts once took place here. Maybe it was not a lost city, but it was undoubtedly a lost civilisation – who had lived here?

We now know that many of these *manda* were built throughout the south in the tenth to thirteenth centuries, hundreds of years before the Tandroy arrived. The ancient people who inhabited them had certainly traded with the outside world – Islamic pottery from the Persian Gulf and celadon porcelain made in China are present in the traces they have left behind. The descendants of the inhabitants of the *manda* had departed by the seventeenth century, and the north of Androy then remained almost empty of people until the mid-nineteenth century, when some of the Tandroy clans migrated into the area to settle there.

Our time was up. We said our goodbyes to the kindly villagers, including our budding archaeologist and his sisters. These little girls had several times succumbed to inquisitiveness and peeked into the mysterious contents of our field bags. A first experience with a torch had baffled the smallest – knowing only candles and paraffin lamps, she had solemnly tried to blow out the light. She also liked looking at our maps although her first reaction to such a big square coloured thing was that it must be some sort of foreign *lamba*. She had gone off wearing one wrapped around her waist until it was retrieved by her mother.

Our long stay had enabled everyone, even the smallest children, to get used to us. They knew what we were doing since they had fieldwalked with us and helped sort the pottery we found. They knew what we were like, having watched our very ordinary daily lives. In subsequent field seasons we have rarely been able to stay for so long in one village. Unlike anthropologists who settle down with their hosts for months or years, our survey work often entails moving from place to place every few days. However much we explain ourselves, no one really gets to know us properly, a state of affairs which was to become a problem in later years.

9

Life as a Slave

When compared to Robert Drury's description of his life in Madagascar in the 1700s, some aspects of the world of the Tandroy seem to have changed very little. Separated in time by three hundred years, we and Drury had mutual misgivings about the food. Drury soon noticed that in terms of diet 'some Beggars in England far'd much better than I did here' but he was less downcast when he realised that slaves and kings alike ate the same food. Drury had arrived from a country where eating habits had recently changed dramatically and were having a profound effect on the rest of the world.

At the time Drury lost contact with his own world, the English common people are said to have been better clothed and fed than anyone else in Europe. Androy had almost none of the things Drury ate at home. Back in Europe, from the New World there came tomatoes, four sorts of potatoes (sweet 'Spanish potatoes', artichokes or 'Canadian potatoes', 'Virginian' and 'Irish' potatoes), turkeys, chocolate and sugar. Pepper, now affordable by most, came from Indonesia and the Malabar coast of India, and coffee was imported from Mocha in Arabia. Many of these exotic foods were still beyond the reach of the labouring classes whose diet was mainly bread, beef, beer and cheese at best – and bread and water at worst. The poor were 'glad of a piece of hanged bacon once a week' and now and again 'a bit of hang'd biefe, enough to trie the stomach of an ostrige'. Tea, shipped by the Dutch and English from China, was creating a sensation even though it cost 10*s* a pound – nearly a week's wages for a craftsman. Poor Drury wouldn't get another cup of tea for nearly fourteen years.

Another import Drury never came across was manioc; although it is now the Tandroy's staple food, manioc originated in South America. It was already being grown in West Africa in the early eighteenth century, but it had apparently not then reached Androy so Drury never had to eat the stuff (he didn't know his luck, in our opinion). Like us, Drury ate both dried meat *kitoza* and *pitsoke*, the blood and fat fast-food stew. The beef should have kept him happy. Monsieur Misson, a French gourmet who visited London in the early 1700s, was very taken by the English obsession with beef and even met people who rarely ate bread, such was their love of meat. Fast food was already thriving in London: on Cooks' Row near the river Monsieur Misson observed cookshops with four spits, each carrying five or six joints of beef, pork and mutton, from which slices were served with salt, mustard and a bread roll, accompanied by a bottle of beer. Perhaps Drury found *kitoza* a reasonable substitute for a take-away kebab.

Drury spent much of his slavery as a cattle herder. He struggled with his new job at first. Although Britain in 1703 was predominantly an agricultural society, with about 70 per cent of the population of 5.5 million involved in farming, he had grown up as a city boy and then spent two years as a sailor, so he had trouble managing the unruly and nimble cattle. He thought them the biggest he had ever seen although today they look very skinny. (British cattle look in comparison as though they have been over-inflated with a bicycle pump up the bottom.) He remarked on the fatty humps of these zebu and on their wonderfully coloured skins, and noticed that the cows provided only a little milk.

He describes the heavy tails of the Tandroy fat-tailed sheep and says how he thought they looked very like goats. We still have the same trouble. Being used to the fat and fluffy white sheep of Britain, we have to work hard to sort the sheep from the goats in Madagascar. The distinguishing characteristic we eventually learnt to use is that goat ears stick up, sheep ears hang down. Interestingly, archaeological specialists in animal bone have great difficulty in telling apart the remains of sheep from those of goats. The two species are skeletally almost identical and, in many parts of the world like Androy, very similar in appearance today.

Drury tells us that the Tandroy had only small numbers of goats, in contrast to today when goats seem to do much better than sheep in the arid climate and prickly vegetation of the south. Tandroy sheep seem to suffer from perpetual head-colds and one wakes in the morning not just to crowing cocks but to the sound of runny-nosed sheep sneezing wetly. Drury also observed that the Tandroy had a taboo on raising or eating pigs, just like today, and that only 'the very Refuse of the People' ate them.

Everywhere in Madagascar people live with taboos (*fady* or, in Tandroy dialect, *faly*). Taboos are a serious thing and should be respected by outsiders. *Faly* also translates as 'sacred': all tombs and their environs are *faly*, as are certain patches of forest. When we are surveying for sites one of the pieces of information we must seek out before going into the fields is which areas are *faly* and therefore must be avoided. It can be inconvenient and frustrating but there is no point trying to argue – we are there on sufferance and must obey the rules.

Many taboos, like the avoidance of pork, are dietary prohibitions. The Tandroy live in a landscape inhabited by wild creatures, most noticeably tortoises and lemurs, but both these creatures are *faly*. They do not hunt, eat or even touch them. There are other animals which no one eats – like us the Tandroy wouldn't dream of eating a dog or a cat unless facing starvation – but these are not *faly* in the same way as tortoises.

At first we thought taboos were a matter so serious that they should be discussed only in tones of great solemnity, but over the years we have discovered that Retsihisatse puts up with a lot of teasing from our other Malagasy colleagues about his *faly*. We have seen Ramil chasing him round the Landrover brandishing a large tortoise, both men in fits of laughter, but they trust each other not to go too far.

Victor, our mechanic in later field seasons, is from the Antemoro people of the east coast and takes his taboos much more seriously. Ramil once made us sit on and hide a roasted tenrec we had been eating when Victor arrived unexpectedly. The hedgehog-like tenrec is one of his major taboos and he would have been most uncomfortable to be in its presence. Ramil, on the other hand, seems prepared to eat anything – bat, cat and tortoise have all passed over his plate – and flatly refuses to tell anyone what his *faly* are.

The most important animals to the Tandroy of both the eighteenth and the twenty-first centuries are their cattle. Men love their cattle and treat them with respect, but otherwise people's attitudes to animals are often very unlike our own. The various taboos protect some wild creatures, but whether animals might suffer and feel pain is of little concern. This is not just a Tandroy quirk but a fact of life everywhere in Madagascar. On a journey north one year we drove for miles behind a grossly overloaded cattle truck. The drivers must have had trouble squeezing in the last few animals so one beast was travelling with its rear end in the air, hoisted off the floor by its tail which had been knotted around a slat in the lorry's side.

Drury makes no comments at all on such things; eighteenth-century English attitudes to animals were probably fairly close to those of the Tandroy. For our part, we had never lived in a community that relied so completely and intimately on its animals and found it difficult to wring the neck of a chicken, let alone cut the throat of a cow.

As well as animal herding, the Tandroy cultivate some crops; in Drury's day most field labour was performed by slaves, and today it is primarily the responsibility of women. One day early in his captivity Drury was taken to the bean fields with the other slaves and given what he calls a hoe (actually a *fangaly*, the Malagasy flat-bladed spade) with which to dig up weeds. He probably wasn't much interested in vegetable gardening – back home in London vegetables and fruit of many varieties could be bought in the square at Covent Garden, but they were not particularly popular. Vegetables were thought to cause flatulence and fruit was eaten mainly 'to keep down the vapours'. Drury feigned ineptness in the fields and was put to work with the cattle, which he liked better since he had the company of other boys.

Then as now the herd had to be driven daily the long distance from their pen inside the village to the ponds and Drury had to bring home a large tub of water for the household. It was his job to make sure that the stock stayed out of the fields and did not eat the crops. For the boys who watch over the animals today this is still the major responsibility. Not surprisingly, Drury sounds as if his heart was never really in his work. If manioc had been growing, he would have been in deep trouble with his straying herds as the leaves are poisonous to cattle. Every now and again in the dry season, starving cattle eat the enticing greenery of manioc plants and have to be force-fed an emetic to save them.

In Drury's early days of slavery his master went away to war. The Tandroy not only had uneasy relations with their Tanosy neighbours to the east but were also in permanent conflict with the Mahafaly who lived to the west. These two groups were (and still are) very similar in language, culture and appearance and so hated each other implacably. Within a year of Drury's arrival in 1703 the Tandroy were on the march against the Mahafaly. Some short time before, the Mahafaly had killed the father of the Tandroy king and Kirindra was bent on revenge. Drury's master was one of King Kirindra's grandsons and therefore left his home village to go campaigning against the Mahafaly king named Hosintany.

Drury's book about his adventures in Madagascar gives the names of all the people he met and heard about, written down phonetically: King Hosintany of the Mahafaly turns up in Drury's book under the delightful name of Woozington. The phonetic spelling of many of the Tandroy words in *Robert Drury's Journal* seemed rather distant from their real spelling and pronunciation today until we realised that Drury must never have lost his strong London accent. The *Journal* reveals how a true Cockney would have said these words, not necessarily how the Tandroy pronounced them!

Drury wrote about a conflict between 'Woozington' of the Mahafaly and 'Crindo' of the Tandroy. Nearly two hundred years later, the tale of this war was still being told by the Tandroy. The French ethnographer Emile Defoort, writing just after 1900, heard and wrote down a story which said that the cause of the falling-out between the two kings was an argument about cooking. Hosintany and Kirindra were hunting together and killed a wild boar. When it came to cooking their catch, Kirindra had been unable to light a fire. Reluctant to own up to his ineptitude he had promptly declared that wild boar was taboo for him and his people, and the two men had argued bitterly.

Whether the true cause of the war was the murder of Kirindra's father or a spat about fire-lighting, it led to a great battle. Hearing that the Tandroy were on the move against him, attacking his people's villages, the Mahafaly king mustered an army of three thousand warriors and advanced towards the Tandroy capital at Fenoarivo to meet his foes, a force of two thousand men led by two of Kirindra's sons. Hosintany and his men routed the Tandroy and fought their way into Fenoarivo, burning it down after they had plundered it. Drury is uncertain about the later course of the war and how a cease-fire was arranged but the Mahafaly eventually broke off their campaign, leaving Kirindra to rebuild his shattered capital.

Drury loathed his master Miavaro, an evil-tempered and violent man who frequently threatened to kill his little red slave, and was glad to see the back of him when Miavaro left to fight for his grandfather. Robert remained with his master's wife, herself a slave, the captured daughter of a king in the north, who showed him much kindness. While Miavaro was away, she took him to visit one of the other *Degrave* survivors who was being kept at another village a few miles away. The two boys bemoaned their fate, reduced to wearing only loincloths ('arse-clouts' to the vulgar English sailors) and suffering from blistering sunburn.

Drury tells how he was obliged to lick his master's feet when Miavaro returned from battle; he tried to refuse at first but

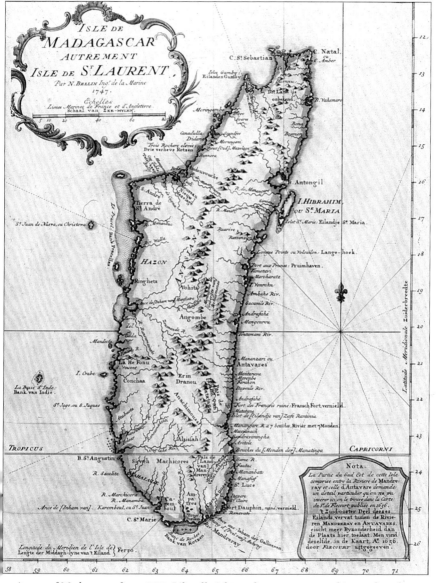

A map of Madagascar from 1747. Like all eighteenth-century maps, this was based on Flacourt's map of 1656.

The wreck of the *Degrave*, an engraving from *Robert Drury's Journal*.

The project team with the cannon on the reef at the shipwreck site.

Typical landscape in the spiny forest: *fantiolotse* trees, cactus and aloes.

A boy coming home from the waterhole to a village near Mionjona, the area where Robert Drury was kept as a slave.

A Tandroy stone tomb from the earlier half of
the twentieth century.

A recently built Tandroy stone tomb with paintings of scenes
from the occupant's life.

After the cattle have been sacrificed, the coffin is manoeuvred into place for burial within an existing stone tomb.

Beside the tomb, women wail under their *lamba* as the coffin is buried.

During a funeral, the kinsmen of the deceased stampede the cattle through the village to show off the family's wealth.

Tandroy children fieldwalking at Ambaro to collect
ancient pottery sherds.

After a thunderstorm, the children of Mionjona watch the team excavating a trench through the defences of Robert Drury's village.

Fieldwalking among the sand dunes west of the Manambovo rivermouth.

Ramilisonina with the egg of an Elephant Bird (*Aepyornis maximus*).

Retsihisatse (left) with our Mahafaly guide in the dunes at the mouth of the Menarandra river.

Miavaro was prepared to kill him for his disobedience. Nobody licks feet any more in Androy but in the Tandroy dialect it still survives as a metaphor used as a term of affection and respect by wives to their husbands.

In the rainy season Drury was sent away with three other boys to live out in the pastures with about two hundred cattle. His mistress gave him an 'earthen Pot to warm my Milk in, a Callabash to drink out of, and a Mat to lye upon' and his master supplied him with an axe, a spear and a new *lamba*. All these items are still basic household goods today, with the exception of pottery which has been replaced by plastic and aluminium. During the torrential downpours of the rainy season Androy can feel terribly cold and Drury even calls the rains 'winter' though it is technically summer in the southern hemisphere. The boys huddled together for warmth in the leaky little house they built for shelter.

The cattle herders' only food, other than a little milk, was quails which they caught in traps, so the hungry boys worked out ruses to kill the odd cow in secret, but they were eventually caught. Drury's three companions were castrated on the spot by their masters, but he pleaded with Miavaro to be spared this treatment. The alternative punishment was to be shot: his master tied him to a tree and fired a musket at him from a distance of 80 yards. Fortunately he missed and released the boy.

So after about two-and-a-half years with the cattle, Drury was sent back to the fields in disgrace, with the threat of castration hanging over him. If incompetent weeding resulted in his digging up the crops again, he was going to be in big trouble. The fields in which he laboured were 5 miles from home, at a healthy distance from the evil Miavaro, and Drury also had his own plot on which he could work for one day a week. Getting started was difficult and Drury reckons he would have starved without the wild yams he gathered in the forest and food given to him by his fellow slaves. He must have been ravenous most of the time: back in England people ate often and in vast quantities. The typical English lunch was a formidable affair of roast mutton or beef *and* mutton pie or roast chicken *and* bread and cheese, all washed down with beer and wine. The French gourmet Misson was amazed at the size and duration of these lunches, where people ate until they had 'quite stuff'd their Paunch'. Supper, in contrast, was a light meal: the English were 'gluttons at noon, and abstinent at night'.

Drury's greatest success in the next few years was with bees and the English–Tandroy dictionary at the back of his book reveals an intimate knowledge of beekeeping. For example, the Tandroy word for drone, *renetantely vazimba*, is specific to their dialect and crops up in his lexicon as 'Ferzimber'. He describes the Tandroy techniques which he used in beekeeping:

> Theres little Trouble in the Management of Bees, which are here very numerous; they will readily come to their Hives, or *Tohokes* [*tohoke*], as the Natives call them; and I took a particular Delight in making them: They are Part of the Body of a Tree, call'd *Fontuoletch* [*fantiolotse*]; which is first cut off about a Yard long, and then split right down: After we have dug out the Middle with our Hatchets (in which Operation we are not over nice) we bind the two Parts together in their natural Position, so that the Hive is a hollow Cylinder; we leave a hole at the Bottom, for the Bees to enter: And this is all the Care that need be taken.

Hives are still made exactly this way today, although honey is less important now that sugar cane can be imported for making rum. Nonetheless, hives are still carefully guarded in special beehive forests. For Drury honey was valuable since he could trade his produce with the Tandroy rum-makers. He also had trouble with honey thieves, but even though he was a slave he still had rights over his own property and managed to get compensation – two axes, a spade and ten strings of beads – from the father of one thief whom he caught red-handed.

Drury makes no complaints about drinking rum – the years on the *Degrave* had probably given him a taste for it. In England spirits were a relatively recent innovation, just becoming accessible to all with half a million gallons of Dutch genever gin being imported each year. There was also whisky, imported rum and a nasty 'British brandy' in the absence of the French original, off the menu because of the wars with France.

Drury must have missed the beer, though. Misson tells us that the English brewed 'a hundred and a hundred sorts of beer and some not bad' but just how much people drank is hard to say. Everyone drank weak 'small beer' in preference to contaminated water; records surviving from Christ's Hospital in London show that the weekly order of beer was enough to provide each inmate with three pints a day. Drury had also said goodbye to West Country cider, Portuguese wine and the sweet Madeira and Canary wines. Again, the quantities drunk seem unbelievable – in London taverns in the early 1700s the smallest serving measure for wine (a nipperkin) was half a pint and the standard measure was a quart, more than a bottle and a half.

Drury recounts a lengthy story of how he conspired with his master Miavaro to protect some beehives with a magic potion. A passing *ombiasa* (a diviner and astrologer) agreed to mix up a poison to sprinkle on the hives. They spread a story that any thief who touched the hives would suffer from red spots on the skin and a bloated stomach, and would then die unless a secret antidote were drunk. Drury acted as the fall-guy. Master and slave let it be known that Drury had stolen honey from Miavaro's magic-protected hives. Drury nipped behind a bush, pretending he needed to relieve himself; while no one was looking, he whipped up a rash on his own body with 'nettles' – in Androy there grows a stinging nettle tree – and drank quantities of milk to swell his stomach. His play-acted affliction convinced everyone that the magic was effective and the beehives were safe from then on. For Drury's part in this little conspiracy Miavaro rewarded him with a cow and a calf to call his own.

It is hard to tell how much Drury believed in the various types of magic used by the Tandroy. The world in which he grew up was only just shedding its own faith in such supernatural powers. The old beliefs and superstitions were fading, but not yet gone. Prosecutions for witchcraft had only come to an end two years before Drury's birth: the last person in England to be executed for witchcraft, the unfortunate Alice Molland of Exeter, was hanged in 1685. In the English countryside, suspicions of witchcraft still arose; accused women were occasionally subjected to 'swimming' and might even drown as local communities took the law into their own hands. Tandroy magic may not have seemed too far-fetched to the young Drury – he came from a city whose inhabitants believed astrologers could foretell the future and, most importantly, find lost property, from spoons to sheep to 'clothes stole off the hedge'!

One of the strangest aspects of Drury's servitude is that, after he had gained his master's trust, he was appointed to sacrifice cattle at ceremonies. He relates that cattle could be killed only by men of the highest rank and, although he was a slave, he was thought to be the son of the deceased Captain Young and thus of high status. He was soon going around as a ritual slaughterer, cutting throats for the useful fee of a large piece of beef. It is hard to find out much about the men who officiate at sacrifices today; the topic is delicate since the funerary priests who cut up the cattle slaughtered at funerals are probably descended from slaves.

Slavery or serfdom existed throughout Madagascar in the past and was only suppressed after the coming of the French at the end of the nineteenth century. In most ethnic groups there is continuing prejudice against people of slave descent. In Androy clans with a slave ancestry often live in quite poverty-stricken villages alongside the flourishing settlements of their ancient masters, with whom they have a relationship marked by continuing inequality and subservience. But it is terribly difficult to ask questions about how the system worked in the past and what its consequences are today. Over-inquisitiveness causes enormous offence. Only after ten years of friendship with Retsihisatse did he finally tell us about the families whose ancestors had once been his own clan's serfs.

The English boy Drury was growing up into a Tandroy man and became trusted enough to be given a gun and taken hunting for wild cattle. These were humpless, and quite different from the domestic zebu. They used to be found throughout southern and east Africa, where David Livingstone was one of the few Europeans ever to see them. There are no wild cattle left in Madagascar today but they are still remembered by the Tandroy. The other favourite hunt quarry was wild boar, which do still live in the remote forested areas of Androy.

Other animals seen by Drury are what he calls 'foxes' (actually the *fossa*, a slender carnivore which occupies about the same ecological niche as the European fox) and 'turtles' (in Drury's day 'turtle' in English was interchangeable with 'tortoise'). He describes the scorpion as 'the only venomous Creature I ever saw there' and mentions 'pretty little Lizards', perhaps referring to the fact that some lizards in Androy have blue and green tails or maybe to chameleons. Drury has no word for lemur and refers to them as 'Monkies', but then he lived in a pre-Linnaean world and classifies fauna and flora mainly in terms of their edibility or danger! He does not mention fleas or lice at all, probably because these were a taken-for-granted nuisance in Androy and in England, where we know people sometimes spent an evening 'overhauling their shirts and pressing their eight-legged enemies to death between their thumb-nails'.

Drury carefully describes the hemp plant and the effects of smoking cannabis but did not have an English word for it, calling it 'Jermaughla' (*jamala*). He didn't like it at all, since it made him 'so very giddy'. Cannabis, also called *rongony* in modern Tandroy, is still grown today for personal use and sold in small quantities, as is tobacco. Being caught selling either will lead to arrest and a fine; we have never discovered whether the purchaser is also committing an offence. Just as in Europe, growing and smoking cannabis is an activity that involves a degree of discretion and many older people disapprove of it. The local tobacco, plaited into sticky brown ropes, is usually chewed but occasionally smoked, rolled in maize leaves or scraps of school exercise books. In Drury's time both *jamala* and tobacco were smoked in pipes made of reeds or occasionally very long shells. Drury would have been familiar with pipe smoking – the Dutch were bigger smokers than the English but the trade was flourishing on both sides of the Channel. We sometimes find stone pipes on archaeological sites in Androy. They are definitely of local manufacture – their design is unlike anything ever used in Europe – but they date only to the nineteenth century.

After spending years working in the fields, Drury was put back on cowherd duty. He was now a grown man, about twenty-one years old, and had his own tiny herd of one cow, two heifers and a calf. He soon lost everything. One evening on the way home from the waterhole the cattle herd was attacked by a gang of armed men. These cattle rustlers were led by two of Miavaro's uncles. The royal dynasty was racked by feud and the English boy Robert Drury was about to become a Tandroy warrior.

Crime and Violence

Conflict had been brewing between the king and his closest relatives. Kirindra's nephew Mananjaka, who had a strong claim to the kingship, was an immensely popular man, much to Kirindra's chagrin, and had a powerful faction on his side. Drury admired this 'intrepid warrior' enormously, considering him to be 'just, honourable, generous, and of a courteous Disposition'. As well as a rumbling disagreement over the royal succession other tensions were at play. A series of cattle thefts involving the royal family were becoming more and more violent. At this point Drury's status changed: he may have been a slave but he was still expected to fight like any other man. He was given a gun and went into battle.

Miavaro took revenge for the loss of his cattle herd by leading his men in a brutal dawn raid on his uncles' village, where they took captive many women and cattle. They plundered the village and razed it to the ground but the wicked uncles were far from beaten. At daybreak the following day came a swift counter-attack on Miavaro's village. The women, children and captives were ordered into hiding in the forest just in time but Miavaro had to retreat under the onslaught, leaving four dead and many wounded. It was at this point that Kirindra, father and grandfather of the quarrelling parties, intervened to arrange an amnesty.

Miavaro would not agree to make terms. Foreseeing the consequences of his refusal to parley, he evacuated his village, sending everyone to seek shelter at the home of a relative half a day's walk away. Drury describes packing for the evacuation – his pathetic belongings amounted to a mat, an axe, a small spade and some dried beans. To punish Miavaro for his insolence, Kirindra's forces burnt down the abandoned village, tore up its crops and took any stored produce left behind. Kirindra's men marched after Miavaro and besieged the village where he had taken refuge with his people, all of them holed up inside the village defences with the cattle, some of which were wounded and causing mayhem. Unable to storm the village by force, Kirindra resolved to starve them out. They had not had time to collect water before the attack and were soon desperately thirsty: 'This Want of Water is the most intolerable of all Calamities, a painful Misery not to be express'd in Words.'

When the siege was lifted Miavaro's people headed home and set about building a new village, searching out 'a Wood so thick, that a Dog could not creep into it' and then cutting a clearing within it. The living defences were further fortified with immense tree trunks set into trenches to form three or four palisades around the village. Entry was through a single gateway defended by four consecutive entrances. The only other access was a secret escape route for the women, children and slaves. In our most recent excavations we discovered the site of Miavaro's rebuilt village, once ringed by palisades which only survive today as stains in the soil.

The plot against the king thickened when Miavaro entered into an alliance with the rebel prince Mananjaka and other members of the royal clan were drawn into the conflict. With war in the air the cattle had to be protected at all costs and Miavaro decided to send part of his herd off to the west to seek refuge in Prince Mananjaka's home territory. Drury was part of the armed guard detailed to escort the animals on a tortuous journey around the north of Androy and down the Manambovo river. This route led the cattle train first to Angavo, the mountain-top village of Mananjaka's younger brother, and then onwards to the foot of Vohimena, the Red Mountain. Drury describes it as shaped like a sugarloaf – a good description of its steep sides and distinctive rounded dome of a summit – and says he thinks it was the highest mountain in the whole of Madagascar. Vohimena is actually small in comparison to the mountains of the far north but it is certainly the highest point in Androy, towering 500m above the flat plains. From Vohimena the herdsmen headed south-west into Mananjaka's territory. Here Drury spent the rest of the war in comfort and safety, with little work to do since he had plenty of help in looking after the evacuated animals. News of the progress of the fighting arrived from time to time.

Many months later, about a year and a half after the outbreak of hostilities, Drury drove the cows back home along the same route. It was not long before Miavaro's uncles, his old antagonists, sent a war party of two hundred men to ambush the herd. Drury was the only cowherd on duty – he was considered expendable since he had no friends or relatives – and he evaded death only by plunging into a dense thicket, a painful hiding-place since he was punctured by the spines and prickles. Other men came running to repel the attack and save the herd and when the fighting moved away, one of the enemy warriors lay wounded nearby. Drury emerged from hiding and killed him with one of the man's own spears.

It is no surprise that Drury took to a soldier's life with gusto since throughout his life he had lived in dangerous and desperate places. Actual warfare may have been a new experience, but even back in London as a boy he had lived in an atmosphere of violence. He grew up in wartime – the endless conflict with France – and the peace which had come in 1697, when he was ten years old, was probably even worse. Some hundred thousand soldiers and sailors were left out of work with the onset of peace and the crime rate had rocketed. The lower classes of London became the 'mob'. Footpads roamed the streets, servants stole from their employers and mounted highwaymen lay in wait on the roads out of the capital.

In Drury's youth in London a clamp-down on crime criminalised the wicked and the desperate equally. Prisons were crowded and the gallows were busy providing public executions for crimes against people and property. House-breaking and shoplifting of goods over a value of 5s were capital offences. Out of thirty-eight men and women indicted for shoplifting between 1699 and 1701, seven were sentenced to death. There were three or four hanging days a year at Tyburn (near present-day Marble Arch), where crowds gathered to see the twitching 'strugglers' throttling on the ends of their ropes. The brutalities of life in Androy may not have seemed so shocking to a boy hardened to such sights.

Punishment of offenders could be cruel in Androy – Drury himself had narrowly escaped castration as a boy – and it was positively brutal in England, where convicted felons were branded on the face, on the left cheek next to the nose, so that they would be readily identifiable. A petition from the City of London to Parliament did point out that this was not having the intended effect as first offenders were made unemployable for life! Convicts pardoned from a death sentence might be transported to the colonies in America but for branded prisoners released on to the streets the only option was to pursue a life of crime. Ranged against the criminals, in an age before policemen, were the armed turnkeys of Newgate gaol, constables of the watch and informers. Professional thief-takers earned their living as bounty-hunters, tracking down villains for the rewards paid by the authorities. The conviction of a highwayman, for example, was worth £40 – more than a year's average wages.

Since reaching Androy Drury had lived in a world riven not by daily crime but by incessant feuding. The violent clashes had now brought the entire country to the brink of famine but, luckily for all, outside arbitration arrived in the form of an ambassador from the king of the Fiherenana, a region on the west coast. This king was at war with the Mahafaly people on their western border – Mahafaly country lay to the south of the Fiherenana – and was looking for allies. He needed to stop the Tandroy tearing themselves apart so that he could enlist their support to harry the Mahafaly on their eastern flank.

This contact with the people of the Fiherenana brought the first news of the outside world that Drury had heard for many years. The ambassador reported that the king of Fort Dauphin was dead (records show the pirate king Abraham Samuells died in 1708) and that ships rarely stopped there any more. Making contact with this embassy from the west coast put ideas of escape into Drury's mind: if he headed towards the Fiherenana region he might make it to St Augustine, the trading port where English ships called regularly. The ambassador from the west understood Drury's plight and offered to buy him from his master but Miavaro refused to part with Drury even when offered four slaves in his place. Drury went off to the woods and 'wept till I was almost blind'.

Six months later war broke out again against a new foe, Reambaroha, a 'petty Prince to the northward'. Drury was given a musket, two gunflints, twenty lead balls and some powder and set off in a war party of three hundred men. Reambaroha's village turned out to be an easy target for a dawn attack. Drury seems to have been confident in his new life as a man at war since he made straight for the prince's house and captured his wife and her attractive daughter, whom he judged to be about sixteen. Miavaro allowed him to keep the captive of his choice so Drury chose the girl and presented his master with the mother, a woman in her thirties, whom Miavaro returned to Reambaroha. Drury roped his 'pretty Prisoner' to him and the victorious warriors set off home.

Drury was evidently very taken with this 'Zorzer Ampeller' (*zaza ampela*, a girl), whom he intended to make not his slave but his 'Walley', his *valy* or wife. From several passages in Drury's book and in earlier histories from the failed French colony at Fort Dauphin it is evident that capture was a perfectly acceptable way of acquiring a wife – Miavaro's own wife, for example, was herself a prisoner. Drury suspects his audience might feel uncomfortable about another matter. It is not the brutal wife-capture which he discusses but skin colour: 'Some of my Readers will, perhaps, wonder how I could so passionately love a black Woman; but let them consider, I had been several Years in the Country, and they were become natural to me.'

To the modern eye, there is no wonder in it at all. He is a young man who has just won himself a girl by the traditional means and is obviously quite enchanted by her. Drury describes his teenage wife as 'extremely handsom, of a middle stature, very straight, and exactly shap'd', with regular features and soft, fine skin. His delight in her appearance sounds entirely natural to us in the twenty-first century: Malagasy women are both elegant and graceful.

Drury comments frequently on Tandroy women's modesty, fidelity, good nature and submissive behaviour to their husbands, adding that European women 'come far short of them'. Just how submissive did the young Drury want a woman to be? Back in Britain, in the world in which he had grown up, women at this time had no rights over their inheritance, their property, their offspring, or even themselves. The legal status of British women was similar to that of children and they were perceived as chattels whose duties revolved around childbearing and family life in the patriarchal household. Wives could be physically punished by their husbands, recaptured if they ran away and even incarcerated by them. Perhaps that explains why 40 per cent of all adult Englishwomen were unmarried!

Sexual promiscuity was seen as a threat to the social order and the subject of female chastity was a favourite for sermonising. In 1700 over a thousand London women were convicted of 'lewd and disorderly behaviour'. This invariably referred to prostitution. Those women who ended up in Bridewell prison were publicly flogged half-naked, to the delight of gentleman onlookers. The sexual underworld of London may have changed very little: some men were 'flogging-cullies' who found their 'beastly ecstasy' through paying girls to whip them; 'bull-factors' could be picked up near St James's Park by a woman looking for a gigolo; in the crowd at the Royal Exchange 'buggerantoes' ogled young men.

British women married quite late, at around twenty-four on average – much later than Tandroy girls either in Drury's day or in modern times – and comparison of the marriage registers against the records of births reveals that a large number of brides were pregnant on their wedding day. There was a high rate of illegitimate births. Today in Androy there are no illegitimate children. The concept is impossible in Tandroy society. Any man is pleased to acknowledge a child as his own and, given the fluidity of marriage, many mothers are 'unmarried' at some point in their lives.

Prostitution is another concept that means little to the Tandroy, for whom sex nearly always involves money. Tandroy boys are absolutely obliged to give their girlfriends not romantic red roses but presents of hard cash – to quote the anthropologist Sarah Fee: 'No self-respecting rural Tandroy woman today will consent to sexual relations without a gift of money', a complete reversal of western mores for courting couples. If her lover is stingy or tries to slope off without paying, a woman is entitled to seize his *lamba* from him and make a public fuss until he makes amends.

Drury is coy about his sex life but does mention that during the years of war he often lived at close quarters with women whose husbands were away fighting. Although he insists on how trusting the absent husbands were and how chaste and innocent the ladies, he does also work out that were a half-white baby to appear, it would rather 'point out the Father'!

Despite Drury's affection for his young wife, he clearly desired his liberty more. Had he been living in any other part of Madagascar as a free man safe from the humiliations of being Miavaro's slave, Drury might have stayed. He hoped that the girl would let him take her home to her father's village but she was too frightened to leave, bound by the magic which prevented slaves from escaping. So, although Drury was reluctant to leave his wife behind as a slave who would suffer after his disappearance, he was determined to get away. The rainy season was about to end and he was ready to run. The ambassador from the Fiherenana had described the route to the west and on his travels during the civil war he had once visited what was now his first destination – the mountain of Angavo, two days' walk away.

Angavo is a remarkable place. In his book Drury's odd phonetic spelling turns the name into 'Yong-gorvo', but he describes it perfectly: a white cliff looking like land seen from

20 miles out to sea. Today this mountain is covered by one of the few areas of dense forest left in Androy. Its slopes and flat summit possess their own micro-environment of dwarf trees which shelter troops of lemurs. To get permission to go up the mountain to find out what might lie on Angavo's summit, we drove to a tiny village deep in the forest at its foot, intending to stay with a friend of Retsihisatse. We had sent no message ahead of us and yet the young man seemed unperturbed by our arrival, saying nonchalantly that he had been expecting us. It transpired that a *kokolampo* had informed him that we would come. *Kokolampo* are invisible spirits of the rocks and trees who can possess people as well as bring good or bad fortune. This man had personal communication with a *kokolampo* who spoke to him and guided him. We had come to the right man if we wanted to explore Angavo. He had recently spent three months wandering in the forest and living off its products. And yes, there were ancient sites up there. He knew of a stone-walled site on the mountain crest, a *manda*, to which he was willing to take us the next morning.

As we climbed Angavo we hoped that our guide would not hear any more voices in his head telling him what to do – there was always the possibility that he might get a message to have a go at the foreigners with his spear. But we need not have worried. He was keen to show us the mountain and its inhabitants. In the forest at Angavo's foot we saw trees full of *sifaka* (a startlingly rude word to English ears since its correct pronunciation is 'she-fuck'), fluffy white lemurs that dance a curious two-legged sidestep when they jump across the ground. There we also spotted two amorous tortoises, having been alerted to their languid activities by the sound of shell banging against shell with surprising force.

With his axe our guide opened up a nest of wild bees to gather their honey. These tiny stingless bees landed in swarms on our skin to drink the sweat. He also located the sleeping place of a hibernating tenrec, curled up inside a hollow tree-trunk. It was only about the size of a hamster and we watched in dismay as he hit the little creature on the head with his hatchet and then de-bristled it with the blade of his spear. This was to be a treat for his son back at the village, so he popped the naked body into his breast pocket and on we went.

The *manda* was on the southern edge of the main massif and would have had commanding views of all Androy were it not for the fact that it was completely covered in prickly trees. Moving around in the dense vegetation was hot and frustrating. We spent the morning crawling on our stomachs through the spines among startled lizards to locate piles of rocks and low lines of what looked like collapsed stone walls. However, this was definitely not one of the tenth- to thirteenth-century *manda* of the type that we had surveyed on the hills of northern Androy.

For lunch our guide showed us how to find the edible roots of a vine called *fangitse* by tapping the ground with the end of his spear, just as Drury had described: 'instead of digging at the Root, they went half a dozen Yards at least from it, and struck the Ground with the Points of their Lances, to observe where it sounded hollow; and digging there, they found the *Faungidge*.' The flesh of the melon-sized tuber was white and watery and the sensation was like eating a potato-flavoured sponge. We washed our hands after lunch with the squishy interior of a *vontake*, a large spiny *Pachypodium* shrub. The insides of the *vontake* can be hollowed out and the thorns on its exterior scraped off with a spear to make a wooden container; Drury himself stored his precious honey in a 'Vounturk'.

Descending from Angavo's southern summit we found hoofprints and churned-up ground – there were plenty of wild boar somewhere close at hand. Armed only with a spear, our guide often hunted them with his dogs; we sincerely hoped we would not be meeting any. A little further on small clumps of rice were growing wild in natural depressions in the bedrock. Ramil was ecstatic. Like all Malagasy outside the south, he has a deep yearning for rice. Rice is in the Malagasy soul – it expresses their very identity – and these slender green leaves struggling to grow in a mountain puddle made him homesick for his rice paddies in the north.

We had run out of water hours earlier and our guide headed towards a natural well. Unfortunately, we could smell it long before we could see it. Even though this was October and the end of the dry season there was certainly water in it. The only problem was that there was a very dead goat in there too. The water was green and fetid and the stink unbearable. We no longer felt quite so thirsty.

Our last stop was the *kokolampo*'s home, an atmospheric natural arrangement of large rocks, a reed bed and huge trees. There was clear evidence of the *kokolampo*'s presence, we were told, because the wild boar had not eaten the reeds. Karen lost a gold earring somewhere in the vicinity which caused much nodding of heads – there was definitely a *kokolampo* about.

The weather suddenly changed, bringing storm clouds rolling in from the south. To avoid a soaking we hurried down the mountain, with eagles wheeling over our heads. That evening it poured, signalling the beginning of the rainy season. An immovable herd of goats had taken shelter in the unfinished house in which we had slept the night before so we were lent someone's kitchen. It was a rotten night. The little house leaked badly and in the damp we shivered from the cold, kept awake by a cat catching rats, clattering among heaps of calabashes and enamel plates. We dozed off eventually, to be woken again by the door of the house blowing away in the storm. The next day we were invited to inspect the tree-trunk coffins that the villagers were making. They had filled up with the night's rain and formed useful washing troughs – and offered an opportunity to shave for the first time in weeks.

Some years later we revisited Angavo at the end of the rainy season. We had never been to Madagascar at this humid time of year and found Androy transformed into a world lush with green vegetation, very different from the scorched brown landscape of the dry season. We slogged back to Angavo one moonlit night in April, picking up a string of cactus punctures on the meandering track to the village at its foot. We were going up the mountain to have another look at the *manda*, to see what other sites there might be on its long summit, and to visit a cave in which lie buried many of the ancient Tandroy kings. The area near the cave is still used as a burial place by the royal clan and on the night when we arrived a funeral was in progress, the mourners having just reached the mountain after a 10-mile walk from their home village.

Scrambling up towards the *manda* the next morning we encountered the Madagascar attack-wasp. These do not just buzz around being a nuisance but really go for the intruder. Fortunately, their sting is nothing like as unpleasant as that of a northern hemisphere wasp and, after a painful jab, soon subsides. It was another bad day for the tenrec. When we reached the summit, our guide caught and cooked one, spatchcocked on a pointed stick. There was not much meat on our little barbecue but it tasted delicious, its skin 'as brown and crisp as a pig's', as Drury describes it.

We were determined to work out what the *manda* was. Our guide had heard that it had been the hide-out of a notorious villain named Manorotoro – The Crusher – who had terrorised the Tandroy before the coming of the French. Back in the 1930s the ethnographer Raymond Decary wrote that there had once been a Tandroy guerrilla camp on top of Angavo, occupied by anti-French partisans around 1902. We set to work to find pottery and eventually unearthed identifiable sherds which we could date. This mountain top had been inhabited in the eighteenth century. It had been occupied not only by modern bandits and freedom fighters but also by the ancient Tandroy, probably by one of Mananjaka's brothers. Drury had been here.

We battled through the tangled vegetation along the summit looking for further remains but found only a single burial monument, a grave marked out only by a kerb of stones set on edge. The next day we set off into the spiny forest to find the cave of the kings. At the spot where sacrifices are made to the ancestors, we offered our rum. Pieces of broken pottery indicated that people have brought offerings here since the 1600s. Up in the cliff side were clefts and cavities in the scree of massive boulders. Erosion hollows in some of the boulders formed rainwater traps and caverns, and one of these little caves had been used recently, but not as a burial place. Inside were two sets of palm-frond bedding, a small hearth and fire-making sticks – probably the lair of cattle rustlers who still plague this remote region. Not far away was the ancient burial place, in crevices underneath a large boulder. Limestone slabs marked the graves and we were surprised to find the near-complete remains of an eighteenth-century cooking pot.

Working in the area of Angavo also gave us the opportunity to track the northern extent of the ancient kingdom in Drury's day and to see how it corresponded with his account. We found that there was almost no trace of settlement from this period: the frontier of King Kirindra's kingdom had been further south and the village on the mountain had been an outpost in the wilderness. In the 1700s this whole northern zone of Androy was largely uninhabited. Much further north had lived the Bara people and on the edge of Androy we found one of their large villages from the eighteenth century, strewn with gunflints and pottery. According to oral tradition this had been a Bara fort in the no-man's-land between Tandroy and Bara territory.

Most of the northern and western zone of today's Androy was colonised by the Tandroy only in the nineteenth and twentieth centuries and yet, in many parts of it, there are traces of that much earlier civilisation which constructed the great stone-walled enclosures.

What were they? These *manda* were not forts – they could not have been defended against a concerted attack since no wall had ever been much more than waist- or shoulder-height. Were they royal villages – ancient stone versions of the ones that Drury described centuries later – or were they special gathering places where people feasted in memory of the ancestors or for other ceremonies such as circumcision? We have traced a whole network of these stone enclosures spaced at regular intervals along the Manambovo river. Only archaeological excavation can answer our questions about the lives of the first inhabitants of Androy.

Kings and Funerals

Finding the mountain-top outpost on Angavo was easy compared to finding Fenoarivo. We had one place-name – which had turned out to be a dried-up pond – but Drury gave us a number of clues. It was three days' walk from the coast for the barefooted crew of the *Degrave*, and four or five days' walk west of the Mandrare river to which the escaping company had fled in 1703. It was definitely on the sandy plains of central Androy rather than in the northern rocky zone where we started our survey. Drury's estimate of covering 50 miles on the three-day walk inland from the shipwreck site could not be correct since the sandy plateau peters out around 40 miles from the coast of Androy.

On our next expedition we had not only these topographical leads to pursue but also other clues, thanks to the work of Georges Heurtebize, who had been researching the history of the Tandroy royal clan. French by birth, Georges has lived for many years in Androy; he was a good friend of Retsihisatse's deceased father and Retsihisatse counts him as family. Some anthropologists and archaeologists can be extremely territorial about their fieldwork areas, disliking intrusions by other researchers, but Ramil and Retsihisatse assured us that Georges would be delighted to find someone else taking an interest in his beloved Androy. He had already helped an American anthropologist, Sarah Fee, in her research on Tandroy textiles and women's lives. But there was bad news. Georges was about to leave for his annual visit to France and he had a sad message for us: one of his oldest friends, Retsihisatse's mother, had died and Retsihisatse was waiting for us to arrive before holding the funeral. We had to hurry on south.

This time the team was larger. Jean-Luc Schwenninger is a geomorphologist from Luxembourg, fluent in four languages, who specialises in sand, sand dunes and useful gadgets. Over the coming weeks Jean-Luc's rucksack disgorged all sorts of handy bits and pieces. A magician was coming along too. Victor Razanatovo, mechanic, cook and archaeologist, is one of a long line of magic-makers from the Antemoro people of Madagascar's east coast. His own field of wizardry is fixing cars – we have seen him rescue a stranded tourist in the south by mending the sump of the man's vehicle with nothing to hand except a dab of superglue and the silver paper from a bar of chocolate. Victor's skills were to save us many times in the coming years.

Together with Ramil we drove the same long route south. About 20 miles from Retsihisatse's village we were flagged down and told that the funeral had still not taken place. The Tandroy observe a long period of mourning between a death and a funeral. Weeks and months go past, giving the family time to gather their resources to host an enormous celebration. Messages have to be sent across the country to call hundreds of guests together and supplies must be stockpiled since the family holding the funeral has to feed all those attending. During all this time the corpse lies in its house, waiting in a tree-trunk coffin for the big day.

So although Retsihisatse's mother had been dead for three months, he was holding on for our arrival. He knew that we would want to attend the funeral and that we could probably help – discreetly – to bankroll the event. As a mature man with many wives and children, Retsihisatse had to hold a big funeral and it was going to cost him a fortune. We also found out that he wanted to use the Landrover as a hearse. Tombs are often a long way from villages and during the funeral procession the heavy coffin normally travels on a bullock cart. Retsihisatse wanted his mother to be the first Tandroy woman to go on her final journey by car.

Anyway, as the funeral was not for another week and Retsihisatse and his brothers had all the preparations in hand, we could begin work in the meantime. Our first stop was the village where we had stayed the previous year, to deliver gifts and photographs. Here the village president and Madame president had some very bad news. Everyone in Madagascar knows tales about strangers, particularly 'red foreigners', stealing livers and hearts, but a new rumour, just two months old, was spreading throughout Androy. Europeans were chopping off people's heads to extract their brains in an attempt to find a cure for AIDS. We were told in all serious-ness that forty heads had been taken in one town alone.

The tale had started as a suspicion concerning two Frenchmen in a small red car who were ostensibly travelling around Androy to investigate primary education. This certainly seemed strange since there is patently next to none – there are schoolhouses in some villages but rarely is there any pay for a teacher. Our village friends were deeply worried and it was starting to look as though we might not get the chance to search for Fenoarivo. Robert Drury's words came ringing across the centuries: 'having seen no good Ones here, every white Man is look'd upon by them as much a monster, as a *Canibal* is by us.'

People were clearly extremely anxious, even in an area where most had seen us before. We decided to report in straight away at the local government office in case things turned nasty. The meeting with the officials was very positive, especially as they knew of a possible source of information. They suggested we should visit an old man called Tsihandatse who might help us in our quest. He was one of the royal clan, not a king like the kings of old but their oldest living descendant. It looked as if we had a new clue so our breakfast the next morning was to be a real treat – a slap-up English breakfast. Well, nearly. Rice (one bucketful), corned beef (which becomes the unappetising *corne de boeuf* or 'cow horn' in Malagasy French), and chips fried in washing-up liquid – Victor was having trouble identifying the contents of the plastic bottles in our stores.

Georges Heurtebize has found that all Tandroy clans live in closely defined areas, with the exception of one. The royal clan of the Andriamañare lives scattered in different localities throughout Androy. This is just how Drury describes the political organisation of the Tandroy kingdom: in his day too the royal clan was dispersed into villages spread out across the whole region. Today the largest concentration of Andriamañare is near the dried-up lake which bears the name of Drury's royal village – Fenoarivo – around the village of Ambaro, home of the old nobleman Tsihandatse. Members of the commoner clan who live next to the lake of Fenoarivo told us that their ancestors actually got there first. Their point of departure is long forgotten but, like everyone else, they came out of the east to settle in Androy. They were already living at the little lake when the royal clan suddenly turned up. The great king named Andrianjoma, who reputedly had two thousand slaves, had led his people to this area from the village of Ampotake, far to the south on the Manambovo river, the area which we had surveyed during our first visit. Andrianjoma had fallen out with his brother and headed northwards with his people, eventually settling near the lake of Fenoarivo, promising the original inhabitants that they would enjoy the protection of the royal clan.

It was time to go to Ambaro to meet Tsihandatse, a direct descendant of King Andrianjoma. He was a very old man, still married to two wives, with many children and grandchildren. Older Tandroy rarely know their date of birth but we had learnt from Georges that people can work out their ages from certain key dates in Tandroy history. These are the coming of the French and their Senegalese troops in 1900, the death of the cactus and the resulting famine around 1928, and the great hunger of the mid-1940s. While most of the world was involved in the conflict of the Second World War, many Tandroy died in a terrible drought, unnoticed and uncared for. Madagascar's experience of the Second World War is an odd footnote to history; the island was under the control of the Vichy government and became the only field of battle in which the British army fought against the French. The fighting never reached the south and thus the 1940s are remembered for the famine, not the war.

Tsihandatse was a youth when the cactus died so was certainly in his eighties when we first met him in 1993. He was dressed in the traditional style of loincloth, *lamba* and old-fashioned skullcap hat. His hands were shaky and he could not talk for long without tiring, but seemed quite unsurprised at being visited by a group of foreigners. Ramil outlined to him the history of Robert Drury and he replied that he knew no tales about foreigners arriving by sea. Although Tandroy oral tradition can stretch back hundreds of years, even the oldest histories record only lists of ancestors and not unusual events or stories.

Tsihandatse did, however, know the lake of Fenoarivo, which had been a ceremonial gathering place for the royal clan. Our map was wrong. The pond we had visited (to which the French cartographers had wrongly assigned the name) was actually called *Foetse*, 'tummy-button' pond. This is also the word for that part of a baby's umbilical cord which is taken and buried beneath a special tree. Each branch of a clan has such a tree and regards it as a sacred ancestral place.

Tsihandatse also told us that on the slopes behind his village the fields were full of pottery and that, somewhere out there, was the first village that had been established by his royal ancestor Andrianjoma. There were still several hours of daylight left so, accompanied by the intrigued villagers, we walked up the slope and began looking for sherds. We did not have to look very hard – the ground was littered with them. Even tiny children were soon carrying over handfuls of pottery to our line of fieldwalkers, so much that we had to explain that they should pick up only rims and decorated pieces. It is from these parts of broken pots that archaeologists can best establish typologies and work out chronologies of styles. This instruction created a flurry of activity as the youngsters tried to manufacture their own designs on the plain sherds.

By the end of the afternoon we realised that the settlement which had once stood here had been vast but it was neither the ancient capital of Andrianjoma nor Drury's Fenoarivo. This great royal village was no older than the nineteenth century. It had covered a huge area, about half a mile across, and near the centre was an umbilical cord tree belonging to a branch of the royal clan. These umbilical cord trees of the Tandroy were to be a crucial clue in unravelling the history of the royal dynasty and its links with Robert Drury.

As we walked through the village the next day we heard the thuds of a hatchet chopping wood and discovered that someone was making a coffin. The person to be buried was Tsihandatse's sister, although she was not actually dead yet. The old lady was looking a bit poorly so had been moved out of her house into her kitchen hut, so that only this outhouse would have to be burnt down after her funeral.

The next morning we asked permission to go into a nearby sacred forest, said to be the site of a royal village long ago. Tsihandatse allowed us to enter it just once, to do no more than pick up any pottery on the ground's surface, provided that we obeyed the taboos against digging, defecating or collecting wood while in the forest. He told us that it had been the residence of Andrianjoma himself. Later that morning we slipped into the sacred forest, careful to follow Tsihandatse's request that we should not be seen. Walking in almost total silence in an enchanted wood of rustling trees swarming with butterflies, we soon found pottery – of a very different style. This was no nineteenth-century village but something much older. That night we were too excited by the possibility that we had actually found Fenoarivo to sleep easily and lay with our heads outside the tent, looking up at the brilliant southern stars.

The day of the funeral was approaching. We headed home, stopping off at the small village where Retsihisatse's mother had lived as a girl and where Sarah the anthropologist had recently worked for two years. Her friends showed us with pride the fields that Sarah had cultivated and several times pointed out the stile at which she had once dropped a bucket of water. In this landscape such an accident can be a real calamity. These flat plains of central Androy have no streams or ponds. Collecting water can take all day and we marvelled at Sarah's fortitude to have lived here so happily for so long. In later years we excavated an ancient settlement on these plains, near the modern village of Mionjona, having discovered that this was where Robert Drury had lived with his master Miavaro.

The expedition during which we located Miavaro's village was a slog with a surprise ending. We fieldwalked for days across the plains – an uninspiring landscape so flat in places that it resembles a giant golfcourse – and found that at no time in Androy's history had this waterless area ever had more than the sparsest population. We had the usual problems with local farmers who were none too keen on archaeologists. To make matters worse, Retsihisatse came down with malaria, having been on a trip up north, and then someone dumped a dead dog in our village lavatory. We found traces of just one early eighteenth-century settlement, in a field of beans tucked up against a sacred forest. There were no others. How would we know if this was Miavaro's home? Eventually Mike remembered his last clue. There was one more place-name in Drury's book.

Although he never names his own village, Drury mentions that 5 miles away lay the village of Mahandrovato, an odd word meaning 'rock-cooking'. The name didn't appear anywhere on the map, so one morning in the Landrover Mike casually asked one of our guides if he had ever heard of it. The man was taken aback. That's an old name, he replied, no one calls it *that* any more. And where is it? Oh, about 8 kilometres from that bean field . . . We dug the site in thunderstorms and rainbows, coating ourselves in orange mud as we trowelled away to reveal the remains of a house and the great palisades that had once protected the villagers from their enemies.

It was an area Retsihisatse enjoyed working in, because he was among his mother's family. On the way to his mother's funeral we met the headman of her native village, reckoned to be about a hundred years old. He was a cheerful man, brimming with fun and still capable of using his *fangaly* on the weeds. He had maintained a house full of old treasures. The house itself is one of the last surviving ones to have elaborate carvings on its façades; Tandroy carving is described by the French ethnographers of the turn of the century but today has almost vanished. Inside was a collection of nineteenth-century English stoneware jugs, a circumcision knife, a carved wooden bed and old pots. But the most intriguing object was a small bronze figurine, an Indian *boddhisatva* from the western Himalayas. There has never been direct trade between India and southern Madagascar so how had this got here? Could it possibly have been one of the small items salvaged off the *Degrave* nearly three hundred years ago?

In Retsihisatse's village on the evening before the funeral, we sat around his mother's coffin and listened to the funeral praise-singers until late into the night. A jerry-can of wine had arrived, brought down specially from the wine-growing region of the highlands, far to the north. We were all drinking it with gusto when Mike noticed that its container was an English one. He wondered whether the jerry-can's symbol of a skull and crossbones meant anything to the Tandroy because the label – 'Poison: under no circumstances reuse this container' – clearly did not. Perhaps it would not just be Retsihisatse's mother's funeral tomorrow. As it was, no one was poisoned by anything other than too much alcohol. In town that morning we heard that the headhunting rumour had changed shape. The chief suspects were no longer two Frenchmen in a red car but three red foreigners and three Malagasy in a big white Landrover. What a surprise!

There followed a terrific three-day non-stop party in which hundreds came from far and wide bringing gifts of livestock, along with money and other presents. Retsihisatse and his brothers had decided to bury their mother in their father's tomb. Tombs often contain more than one interment, with women and younger people being added to existing tombs by digging out a space in the great mound of stones which is enclosed by the tomb walls. But Retsihisatse's uncles (his mother's brothers) were being argumentative about the arrangements and Retsihisatse was having sleepless nights worrying how to placate them – it might cost him an expensive present of one of his finest cattle.

After a night of partying the assembled company escorted his mother, driven at a stately pace by Victor in the Landrover, on the long route to the tombs, and buried her at dusk next to her husband. Before the tomb three magnificent steers, one of them a gift from Georges, were sacrificed, signalling the moment when her grave could be dug. Once the coffin had been manoeuvred into a pit dug through the stone rubble filling the tomb walls, the coffin lid was briefly raised and the colourful *lamba* which had adorned it all day were placed inside. While the women wept beneath their shawls, the men covered the coffin with stones. The family finally severed their links with the dead by holding the end of a long thread attached to the tomb, which was then cut. We walked back to the village in the twilight, where the family burnt down the house in which Retsihisatse's mother had lived.

With the festivities over, we spent the following weeks in a hamlet near Ambaro. At the end of each day's work we cooled down in the refreshing slime of the village cattle pond but everyone began to run out of steam. The levels of lice and flea infestation were becoming less and less bearable. The most annoying type of flea burrows into one's feet to lay its eggs, which have to be picked out with the point of a needle. We were all fed up with digging out these creatures from under our toenails every night and Karen was not well. Our field diary entry for 3 October reads:

I (me, Karen) feel awful which is the most important thing about today from my point of view. My face and teeth hurt and green slime is running out of my nose. I seem to be rotting in the head. Mike, however, thinks finding a lovely site is far more interesting . . .

We also had outside worries. One of Jean-Luc's many gadgets was a little short-wave radio and we occasionally picked up the World Service. Since we would be going home by Aeroflot via Moscow as usual, we were startled to hear one morning that tanks were surrounding the Kremlin and the airport was under fire. We had no idea what was going on but took our minds off it by spending many days prospecting for sites over a large area.

We discovered nearly a hundred ancient settlements. Most were from the nineteenth century but some dated back to the fourteenth, fifteenth and sixteenth centuries. We were now thinking hard about the dates of the great Tandroy king Andrianjoma. He was in power at the end of the seventeenth century but the problem remains that the name he bore in life is likely to have been something other than Andrianjoma, which is his death-name. In other words, this great king who ruled the Tandroy in the late 1600s may well have been Kirindra himself, the one-eyed king of Androy whom Drury met in 1703.

We knew we would need to come back again, to chase up the oral histories still further and to do some digging on the sites that were accessible. Sadly, we would never be able to return to the sacred forest which was said to have been Andrianjoma's residence.

Giant Birds and the Marco Polo Connection

All of us were intrigued by an even more ancient strand of Androy's history: the unfeasibly large eggs of the Elephant Bird. We had read that a single *Aepyornis* egg was equivalent to 240 chickens' eggs – a pretty sizeable omelette. But had any human ever eaten an *Aepyornis* egg or were these outsized ostriches already extinct before the first settlers set foot in the sands of the south? We wanted to find out more about the bird. We had seen our first *Aepyornis maximus* skeleton in Tsimbazaza Zoo in Antananarivo. Nearly 10ft tall, the skeleton towered over us. It looked a real dinosaur, with elephant-sized leg bones and massive feet. Its wing bones were tiny. At the top of a very long neck was a vicious pointed beak quite different from the ostrich's faintly comic duck-bill. This bird looked tough.

The disappearance of the Elephant Bird is merely the tip of an iceberg in terms of the human impact on Madagascar's extraordinary wildlife. The great island is a remarkable place for two reasons. It was isolated from the Asian and African land masses around eighty-eight million years ago, to form its own self-contained evolutionary laboratory. Secondly, its late human colonisation, a mere two thousand years ago, has allowed the survival – so far – of species that would otherwise have disappeared after longer exploitation by humans.

Yet the uniqueness of the fauna and flora can be overdone and Madagascar has always been sufficiently far away for Europeans to tell tall tales about its exotic inhabitants. In 1878 a German traveller circulated a story that he had personally witnessed cave-dwelling Malagasy making a human sacrifice to a man-eating tree. This *Little Shop of Horrors* monster, with writhing tendrils and moving leaves, sounds like an outsized and malevolent pineapple! The story was not publicly dismissed by botanists until 1925.

Centuries earlier, around 1667, Monsieur Ruelle told his readers how, during a hunting expedition from the ill-fated French colony at Fort Dauphin, he had shot a 15ft-long flying dragon with black and yellow scales and enormous horny feet. He claims to have brought back its pelt for the colony's governor, the Marquis de Mondevergue, on whose coat-of-arms this monster features as a giant bird with human arms. The French scholars Claude Allibert and Jean-Claude Hébert think that this story of a winged monster might contain a grain of truth, possibly based on an encounter with an *Aepyornis*.

There are two other accounts by early European colonists of the giant birds of Madagascar, but neither is based on first-hand observation. In the Dutch settlement on Mauritius Ferdinand von Hochstetter met a group of Malagasy who had sailed there to buy rum, carrying it away in eggs 'eight times bigger than those of the ostrich'. Von Hochstetter adds that the Malagasy found these eggs from time to time in reed beds while the bird itself was seen occasionally. Our most reliable source is Etienne de Flacourt, one of the early governors of Fort Dauphin. In 1658 he wrote two books about his observations of southern Madagascar and in his natural history notes included this creature, which he had never seen himself: '*Vouroun patra [vorompatres]*, is a large bird which haunts the Ampatres [his name for Androy], and lays eggs like the ostrich; it is a species of ostrich, those of the aforesaid places [Androy] cannot catch it, it searches out the most deserted places.'

For reasons that nobody knows, the *Aepyornis*'s eggs are attributed today to a bird named *vorombazoho* (listening-bird) although the Tandroy have no stories about this creature from long ago. But there are some very early travellers' tales that might relate to the Elephant Bird. In 1178 a Chinese author, Chou Ch'ü-fei, wrote of a large island in the sea off East Africa where there were birds so large that the quills of their feathers could be used as water-jars. The Arab explorers who sailed to Madagascar and the African coast a thousand years ago made similar reports and around 1298 Marco Polo wrote down a long description of the *rukh* or *roc*, of which only the first sentence can possibly have any basis in fact:

> The people of the island [Madagascar] report that at a certain season of the year, an extraordinary kind of bird, which they call a rukh, makes its appearance from the southern region. In form it is said to resemble the eagle, but it is incomparably greater in size; being so large and strong as to seize an elephant with its talons, and to lift it into the air . . .

Two problems here – no researcher can put much faith in a writer who thinks Madagascar was inhabited by elephants, and, more pertinently, there is no way that *Aepyornis* could ever have flown. An adult male Elephant Bird must have weighed half a ton and the wings are pathetically small. Flightless birds such as *Aepyornis* are known as ratites, which means they have no attachment for wing muscles on their breast-bones.

Remains of *Aepyornis* from over a million years ago have been found in northern Africa, but the bird appears to have survived up to recent times only in Madagascar where, without lions, hyenas and humans, it would have had no predators. There may have been over a dozen species of ratite in Madagascar. *Aepyornis maximus* was the largest and *Mullerornis betsilei* was the smallest at about 4½ft tall.

Their eggshells are especially common in the sands of Madagascar's south and south-west coasts. In Androy the shells are also found below the surface of the modern dunes, embedded in 80,000-year-old sand dunes which have turned to sandstone. In terms of geological and archaeological time the Elephant Birds were around for a long while before dying out quite quickly within a thousand years of people first reaching the island. Until this time Madagascar was also home to dwarf hippos, giant ground-living lemurs and huge tortoises. Like the Elephant Bird, these strange creatures may have survived until the first human settlers disturbed the isolation in which they had evolved. While surveying for sites in Karembola, a little coastal region in the far south-west, just outside Androy, we worked one morning with a man who remembered digging in his youth in the 1930s with French palaeontologists excavating bone beds to find the remains of these extinct creatures. *Aepyornis* bones, however, are rarely found and only turn up far inland, in lake and river sediments.

The vast eggshell scatters in Androy's coastal dunes are probably the remains of Elephant Bird nesting places. The complete absence of their bones from the area suggests that the birds migrated away from the south coast after the breeding season was over, perhaps to seek out inland habitats around freshwater lagoons. Other than that, very little is known about their ecology and behaviour. Like other large, flightless birds, they must have been ground-living and probably ate grasses and other vegetation.

Their ungainly legs suggest that Elephant Birds did not need to be fast-moving; their giantism may have evolved in response to the lack of predators. Like the megafauna that existed in the Americas and other parts of the world prior to human colonisation, their demise seems to be linked in some indefinable way to the arrival of people. Did the first inhabitants of the island hunt down these slow-moving, giant turkey dinners? Or did they kill them off by stealing the eggs to make enormous soufflés and handy containers? Perhaps the birds faced overwhelming competition for grazing from the cattle, sheep and goats brought by the island's first settlers. Another possibility is that the climate became much drier two thousand years ago, altering their habitats, depleting their numbers and thus rendering the Elephant Birds vulnerable to human predation. But these are all theories – we needed to find some evidence that the birds and people were around at the same time.

During a break from our site surveying we headed to the beach, to explore the coast south of the market town of Ambovombe. Being at the seaside was fun. Whales were breaching and slapping their fins against the ocean waters, and birds of prey swooped at us out of the sun. We may have been enjoying ourselves paddling in the shallows but the people living here were not doing so well, struggling to wrest a livelihood from reef fishing and from growing stunted crops in fields that were being covered by drifting sand. The vegetation on this wind-blasted coastline was very different from that inland: grasshoppers swarmed in the undergrowth of dwarf trees and scrubby shrubs that grew out of the salt-lashed sand.

We found many ancient settlements in the dunes, and where the incessant wind from Antarctica had blown great holes in the dune front there were sometimes millions of eggshell fragments. Trowelling the face of a sand dune along its layer of broken eggshells, Jean-Luc found a complete shell broken into hundreds of small pieces. Yet none of these dense scatters of eggshell ever seemed to be in the same places as those where the pottery and burnt stones left by people were turning up. Even if the inhabitants had simply been stealing the birds' eggs, it seemed strange that the shells never ended up on their campsites.

In 1961 the French archaeologist Pierre Vérin, the pioneer of Malagasy archaeology, had found pottery and *Aepyornis* eggshells together in middens (ancient rubbish heaps) when he and the geographer of the south, René Battistini, had excavated a thousand-year-old settlement at the mouth of the Manambovo river. We set up camp in Talaky village, on the east bank of the great riverbed. The river only ever reaches the sea in the rainy season when it is briefly in spate; for the rest of the year its mouth is blocked by a sand bar and we were able to wash in the brackish pond behind the bar and swim in the sea. People were used to the comings and goings of motor vehicles since pick-up trucks would arrive once a week to buy the spiny crayfish caught by local divers to sell to the hotels in Fort Dauphin. Victor cooked us superb meals of seafood bought from the young women of the village who spent their mornings shrimping and fishing in rock pools. He thought the prices were extortionate but we found them heartbreakingly low.

For two weeks we walked to work every morning across miles of dunes, staggering through the soft sand under the weight of our excavation equipment. In the fringe of small beach-front dunes we excavated a series of middens (which mark the location of prehistoric settlements), working every day in vicious onshore winds which blew needle-sharp sand in our faces and made the digging slow and difficult. But we found what we were after.

These little settlements beside the sea at Talaky revealed that the inhabitants had relied almost entirely on the products of the reef. There were fish bones, crab claws and many seashells but no mammal bones or crop remains. The people who lived here may have done so on a temporary or even daily basis, raising their animals and crops inland and coming here to spice up their diets with shellfish. What we really needed to find was there. In a few spots in the eroding middens were pieces of eggshell in the same layer as the remains of cooking fires lit by humans.

Back in Britain, the radiocarbon dating laboratory at Oxford discovered that proof about the extinction of *Aepyornis* was going to stay elusive. We had collected pairs of samples – bits of charcoal from the ancient house hearths associated with pieces of eggshell lying next to the charcoal – so the lab could find out if the dates of the people were the same as the dates of the birds. The results were fascinating and frustrating. In the pairs of samples, the dates of the eggs and the charcoal were never the same. We could not prove that the people had taken the eggs to their campsites. But the oldest charcoal at Talaky was definitely older than some of the eggshell, so we had confirmed that the first settlers here on the coast had lived in a land still inhabited by giant birds which had been roaming the earth for a million years.

We have spent weeks slogging through the difficult terrain of these coastal dunes of Androy, always hoping to find more sites from the earliest periods of Madagascar's prehistory. Yet all of our surveys along miles of coastline and our extensively dated finds from excavations suggest that the extreme south of Madagascar, the region now known as Androy, was not settled at all before about thirteen hundred years ago.

Strangely, along much of the coast, there is no sign that these seashore dunes were inhabited at all in the sixteenth to eighteenth centuries. During that period the Tandroy may have continued to use the resources of the shoreline but seem rarely to have settled close to the ocean. Drury does mention going fishing while he was guarding the cattle herds in wartime exile somewhere on the lower Manambovo river and he liked his seafood, including the 'Sorer-reake', *sororiake* or sea urchin 'as round as a Turnip, and full of Prickles'. Perhaps Drury even visited Talaky on one of his fishing trips.

The Riddle of the Sands

We came home to Britain to find that one of the old ladies in our village had just died. The subdued funeral in a country churchyard was very English, and the complete antithesis of Retsihisatse's elderly mother's farewell to the world which had been accompanied by gunfire, dancing, laughter, drunken hedgerow seductions and the helpless bellowing of dying animals. Little did we know that our next visit to Androy would have more than its share of illness, death and funerals.

With what we had planned for the next field season Jean-Luc was going to be an essential part of the team. He and his gadgets had been a storming success, both with the archaeology and with the hordes of children who gathered every time we stayed in a village long enough for them to overcome their shyness. We were delighted that Jean-Luc was prepared to come back to Androy when he knew what he was in for.

We were intending to stay in Madagascar for months this time and would be doing a lot of digging. Along with Jean-Luc, who has the patience of a saint, we needed someone else who could cope with the exasperations of a typical field season in Androy without sulking or trying to escape. In the close confines of a field team, even the most innocuous habits of one's dearly beloved colleagues can become unforgivable acts of monstrous proportions. We needed another team member whom we all trusted and persuaded Helen Smith, a palaeo-botanist at the University of Bournemouth, to come with us. Helen has only one major quirk, her notorious tendency to travel with a phenomenal amount of luggage. The weight of

Helen's rucksack was fortunately not a problem; the Landrover could take the strain and Helen would be a godsend.

On arriving back in the capital Tana (Antananarivo), delays kept us in the city for weeks. The Landrover needed major repairs while we embarked on prolonged shopping expeditions to buy the host of supplies that cannot be found in Androy. This included an enormous sack of rice, we hoped without too many of the stones that are surreptitiously added by vendors to increase the weight. Both Ramil and Karen have broken a tooth on pebbles in their dinner. We finally got on the road but the Landrover sounded most unwell. It was as weak as a kitten and something was clearly wrong. Days later we limped into the little Tandroy town of Betroka where both Mike and Karen became horribly sick. They eventually recovered but the Landrover never perked up and by the time we reached Retsihisatse's village, we were long overdue.

We had timed our trip to meet up with Georges Heurtebize but he had given up waiting for us and left to work on the museum he was setting up in a nature reserve at Berenty, outside Fort Dauphin. There was more bad news. One of Retsihisatse's daughters was seriously ill, as was her infant son. The baby was to die in six days and the mother finally succumbed a few months later. Stories about headhunters were rife and there had been no rain for seven months. To make matters worse, we four Europeans were taking a new anti-malarial drug named Larium and all but one of us were already wrestling with peculiar physical side-effects and a disabling paranoia caused by the drug.

We really wanted to dig a site just a short distance from Andrianjoma's sacred forest. The settlement we had located here might date to around Drury's time and was a possible candidate for the royal capital of Fenoarivo. It was October and none of the European team had ever been in Androy so late in the year. The intense heat was a nasty surprise and we got up earlier and earlier each day with the intention of finishing work before the temperature soared but this plan soon backfired. Mike had the bit between his teeth and the loyal team worked longer and longer hours, never knocking off at eleven o'clock as he promised each morning. We would arrive back at the village exhausted, to eat the usual bucket of rice for lunch, glued to each other's sweaty skin in a house which was rather too small since no one could bear to sit anywhere near the fire.

Our first trench turned up a few sherds but the only 'features' (traces of buildings or activities visible in the soil) were a series of grooves caused by ploughing. In European prehistoric archaeology ancient ploughmarks in the subsoil can survive millennia but this was quite different. Since the plough was introduced to Androy only in the 1960s, these marks were definitely not very old. As we opened new trenches we realised that just a single recent ploughing had destroyed almost all the archaeological deposits. The only traces left of the houses that had once stood here were rectangular smudges of beige and black soil on the bare ground surface. They had been inhabited between 1500 and 1600 – too early to be Fenoarivo, which Drury had visited in 1703. Here were the remains of a village once inhabited by the ancestors of the commoner clan who were already living around the lake of Fenoarivo when King Andrianjoma arrived with the royal clan in the late 1600s.

On 21 October, the day before we finished digging, it was Jean-Luc's birthday. Birthdays are never celebrated in Androy. People know the day of the week on which they were born because of its significance for their astrological destiny but rarely the actual date. We decided to go with our own traditions and arranged a surprise party. Victor acquired a large turkey and Helen, a cunning cook, made scones. Then, to the delight of the children, we produced party whistles and balloons, squirrelled away since leaving England. Balloons do not last a minute in Androy because of the prickles but the whistles were a great success and even Ramil, usually a cautious party-goer, was tipsy.

We had more digging to do but first needed to renew our visas. Rather than going all the way east to the tourist-friendly town of Fort Dauphin, we made the mistake of tackling the bureaucracy in a little market town where the authorities had clearly never been asked to do such a thing before. We arrived at the Commissariat of Police at first light and the chief of police hunted up some paperwork. Armed with sheaves of passes, permissions and passports, each of us filled in a bizarre multi-purpose form. In a dusty filing cabinet somewhere in Androy lies a record in triplicate of our language abilities, academic qualifications, eye colour and mothers' maiden names. The officer who wrote the visa extensions into our passports was a very nice man but achingly slow. As dusk turned into darkness Ramil went to find a torch to illuminate the page as the policeman carefully formed each letter with his biro. In the meantime Karen and Retsihisatse had spent the day in a queue of hundreds of buckets to buy water brought in by road tanker from Fort Dauphin.

We had finally met up with Georges and spent the next few days exploring the coast together, buying a giant red fish (about the size of a sheep) which lasted for so many meals we were all sick to death of it. Having made a survey of Elephant Bird sites, we had to get digging again. Driving back from the beach along a steep sandy track we were startled by a loud noise. Had Victor put a heavy metal tape on the cassette player? Sadly not – it was the engine blowing up.

When Victor opened the bonnet he winced in distress. His beloved Landrover was in a terrible state, with bent piston rods and cogs missing their teeth. Even a magician couldn't fix this. We were well and truly stuck. Georges and Ramil set off to fetch help and by late afternoon were back with a sturdy lorry of some unidentifiable Chinese make. This towed us to the mechanic's compound in Tsiombe. The mechanic was away, in Antananarivo.

On the bright side, our hosts at the compound welcomed us to stay and – best of all – they had a bathroom hut, a lavatory hole and a tap. After we had reacquainted ourselves with the concept of running water, we set out to hunt for scavengeable spares from the various wrecked vehicles littering the town. Victor not only fixed the Landrover but also gave it back its former strength and we headed off to Ambaro, where we asked Tsihandatse if we could dig in the fields adjacent to King Andrianjoma's sacred forest. For such an undertaking he decided that we must ask for the blessing of the ancestors and that would require a sacrifice, to enable him to communicate with the dead. Now all we needed was an animal to kill.

The appropriate gift to the ancestors was a sheep and someone soon offered us one. Unfortunately we were in a sellers' market and they were naturally asking well above the odds. Retsihisatse refused to pay that sort of money and bargained down the sacrifice to a goat and a chicken. On the evening of the ceremony Tsihandatse sat at the door of his house, summoning up his ancestors. The blood of the animals was sprinkled on our heads as each of us came forward to ask the spirits' blessing. We not only got King Andrianjoma's ancestral thumbs-up for an archaeological excavation but Karen also came away with the promise of seven sons. We divided up the goat for everyone in the compound and had the chicken for supper with fried potatoes, soup and pancakes.

In very hot weather we started digging but the time for another funeral soon came around. You can tell a funeral is in the offing by the sound of gunfire: riflemen are paid to shoot occasional salvoes in the days before the interment and at the ceremony itself. Ramil's ears had become alert to the sound of shots because guns mean funerals and funerals mean lunch.

One of the traditions of every Tandroy funeral is that the meat of the cattle slaughtered at the tomb is for the funerary priest, the *tsimahaivelo*, 'he who does not know the living'. He and his family are attached to, but not kin of, the clan whom they serve and Retsihisatse has occasionally hinted that these ritual specialists are former slaves. The priest and his family cut up the sacrifices on the spot and strangers are entitled to a share of the meat – anyone present who is in no way related to the deceased goes home with pounds of fresh beef. Thus Ramil was always keen that we should pay our respects, for culinary as well as ethnographic purposes, and we nearly lost count of the number of funerals we went to that year.

On this occasion a man of the royal clan was being buried at a nearby village. Retsihisatse is related to the royal clan through a string of marriage alliances and so could not eat the meat – but all the more for the rest of us, said Ramil. We stayed very late while Ramil negotiated for some fillet steak with the funerary priest and drove away in the dark with the Landrover packed to the brim with women and children. The Tandroy attitude to transport is that no vehicle is *ever* full and we went home that night with six people in the front (not counting Ramil and Victor who were sharing the driver's seat) and a multitude in the back and on the roof-rack, all singing Malagasy hymns at the tops of their voices. It seemed strange that they were not Christians and did not have a church – they had taken the bits that they liked from organised religion and left the rest.

The following day we were up before dawn to get back to work. Digging in soft soil we needed to work barefoot, and by 10 o'clock the sand was hot enough to scorch. It was 5 November, Guy Fawkes' Night, and we celebrated that night with a couple of miniature sparklers. In the major towns the Malagasy have their fireworks on 26 June, Independence Day, but most villagers have never seen them so one June we took some fireworks to Androy. A minor cattle stampede ensued but the villagers judged it well worth it.

The next morning Mike, normally one of the last out of bed, had volunteered to be first up for fire-lighting duty. As usual the firewood was damp from the dew and the rest of the team were soon woken by much huffing and puffing over the hearth. There had to be an easier way and Mike wanted to know what cunning traditional technique could be used. In response to being asked for the Tandroy secret of fire-making, Retsihisatse replied that personally he found a good splash of paraffin usually got things going.

For the next seven days we continued digging the ancient settlement, every morning rescuing disgruntled tortoises that had toppled into the trench overnight. Georges went to Fort Dauphin and brought back a sack of bread, which speeded up breakfast since we no longer needed to wait for the rice to cook. One dismal morning we finished the last of the jam; by now we were eating bread that was rock hard and green with mould inside and out.

Filthy and exhausted, we finished work a week later. We had made some tantalising discoveries. Pottery from the excavated houses indicated that people had been living at Ambaro around 1700. There had certainly been a village here at about the right date but was it Fenoarivo? Drury says that the royal capital was once burnt down by the enemy and then promptly rebuilt nearby – we hadn't identified any signs of burning so our site may not be the first Fenoarivo but might well be its immediate successor.

We packed up and held our final dispensing of medicines for the village. There were many ailments for which we could offer nothing but sympathy – tuberculosis, for example, is prevalent – but we did what we could for the usual sore eyes and scabby heads. A young woman whispered the nature of her complaint to Ramil. Stumped by an unfamiliar dialect word, he shouted clear across the village to Retsihisatse for a translation. It was a gynaecological problem and the girl was mortified but Ramil has a good bedside manner and retrieved the situation, insisting that illness was nothing to be ashamed of. Nonetheless, she had surely not wanted the entire village to know.

After the medical session we gave our thank-you presents: money, soap, bottles and tin cans. Rural Madagascar is a present-giving culture and *kado* ('present', from *cadeau*) is one of the handful of French words that have become embedded into Malagasy life. Children ask for *kado* from tourists, of course, but it goes deeper than that. As well as the little extra added to market purchases as a *kado*, there is much exchanging of items between individuals. Although some are outright presents, others, like the animals taken to funerals, are gifts to meet obligations.

Money is a perfectly acceptable present in Androy where the symbolic meanings of gifts are closely tied to real economic benefit. In intimate relations money strangely mimics the use of flowers in the west. At funerals it is not memorial wreaths but offerings of cash from kin and other guests which are displayed as conspicuously as possible. Banknotes are pinned to long canes and waved aloft for all to see (and count), to raise the status of both the giver and the receiver.

Within marriage there are certain circumstances in which the husband owes a gift to his wife, often paid in livestock but sometimes in money. Like the western bunch of flowers on a wedding anniversary, there can be uproar if he forgets or is late. Polygamy has its perils. The Tandroy husband has little choice about the amount of time he spends with each of his wives – he sleeps the night in each wife's house on a closely scrutinised rota system and must pay a penalty if he does not show up at the next wife's house by breakfast time the following morning.

Our next destination was the mouth of the eastern river, the Mandrare, which marks the frontier between Androy and the land of Anosy. Here we hoped to find ancient settlements with *Aepyornis* eggshells as we had at the mouth of Androy's other major river, the Manambovo. But above all we were looking for the site of the *Degrave* massacre, where the escaping crew were slaughtered by the Tandroy. The survivor John Benbow had told the Dutch at the Cape that, after wading up to their necks across the Mandrare where seventeen or eighteen were killed, the crew 'did their best to reach the seashore and escape their pursuers . . . That same night again attacked them on a high sand hill, and shot two of their men.' Drury says that on gaining the east bank of the river the escapers 'had not travell'd above two Miles in this Wood, before we came to a large sandy Plain, to which we could see no End, and here they [the Tandroy war party] determin'd to stop our Progress'.

At the old crossing place over the Mandrare, little used since the construction of a road bridge further north, there is an expanse of light forest on the east bank, which does indeed open out on to a wilderness of sand dunes. We scoured this area of woods and dunes, looking for the smallest clue such as a piece of human bone or a lead musketball. People in the nearby village knew a story about foreigners having been here before the coming of the French so perhaps we were going to be in luck.

But we were looking for a needle in a haystack. Our experience in similar dunes at Talaky had shown that they are very unstable. Jean-Luc is an expert on dune formation and knows that they are fast-changing environments in which the old land surface from three hundred years ago might be buried today under metres of windblown sand. We found a few small pieces of bone on one sand hill but Helen soon identified these as the remains of a sheep or goat.

The day was not entirely wasted however. On the edge of the dunes we picked up pieces of pottery of the seventeenth and eighteenth centuries from the site of a little village occupied around the time of the massacre. Towards the middle of the dune system a group of strange stone cairns poked up out of the sand. Might these cairns have been thrown up over the crew's dead bodies by the Tanosy who came to investigate the fighting on their border? We needed to ask the nearest village for permission to excavate.

We headed for Ambasy, 'the place of the gun', where the villagers had an urgent question – did we have a gun? We protested vehemently that indeed we did not, hoping that they were not worrying about our headhunting proclivities. They were sadly disappointed: a young woman had lost her arm to a crocodile some time before and they were keen to get rid of the beast. We hoped the crocodile wasn't hungry – tomorrow we were going to be wading across the Mandrare up to our chests in water, carrying the excavation equipment.

A crowd of people followed us through the river and joined us on the east bank to see what we might find. We mapped and measured the largest cairn, carefully planning the position of every stone, and began digging a trench into it. By lunchtime we had found only a scorpion and had established that this was a geological formation. We had drawn a blank.

Discussions in Ambasy about the history of the area dashed another hope. The foreigners here before the French had been merchants, probably buying orchil, a lichen used in dyeing. This little colony of traders had been driven out in the late nineteenth century during a minor war between the Tandroy and the Tanosy. We went to see the remains of their settlement and found it littered with a type of English pottery known as 'sponge ware', made around 1860. It was a strange experience. We had seen pottery like this only a few months earlier but thousands of miles away. On the island of South Uist in the Outer Hebrides, where Mike and Helen had been excavating Iron Age and Viking houses, one of their colleagues had been digging a site containing identical decorated pottery. Jim Symonds was investigating the village of Flora Macdonald, the rescuer of Bonnie Prince Charlie. Flora's descendants had used exactly the same 'sponge ware' that we were now finding in southern Madagascar.

The time had come to move on and begin work in a new area. From the valley of the Mandrare we headed west to explore a new landscape, the high plateau in the very heart of Androy midway between the Mandrare and the Manambovo rivers. Leaving behind our hunt for Robert Drury, we were now following another source of information about the early history of Androy.

The Frenchman's Story

Robert Drury was not the first person to write a book about life in southern Madagascar. There is another account, a narration of events over a period of six years, which survives from a time half a century before Drury. In 1648 Etienne de Flacourt was sent out by the *Compagnie française de l'Orient* (the French East India Company) to their military and trading outpost at Fort Dauphin to sort out problems in the colony. Fortunately for today's researchers he was a prolific writer with a keen interest in recording events, customs and natural history.

In 1642 the French had established their first tiny colony of just fourteen men at Baie Sainte Luce, a palm-fringed beach in the south-east corner of Madagascar in the region called Anosy. They soon realised that they had chosen a spot both disease-ridden and dangerous and within a year had relocated to a nearby defensible promontory. Here they built a fort named in honour of the Dauphin, heir to the French throne, a miracle baby born to estranged parents after twenty-three years of childless marriage. Later in 1643 this little prince ascended the throne at the age of four to become Louis XIV, the Sun King.

The first commander of the colony, Sieur Pronis, cemented relationships with the Tanosy rulers by marrying a local girl, a cousin of the king, Andriandramaka. King Ramaka was well disposed towards Europeans, having been educated abroad by the Portuguese in Goa, and Pronis's marriage was a wise move in terms of relations with the locals, but it soon became a source of tension within the colony. The other French residents were unhappy that he appeared to be provisioning his wife's large family from the colony's stores. There also seems to have been a grumbling religious conflict because Pronis was a Protestant and the rest of the settlement were Catholics. In 1646 the colonists mutinied against their governor.

Pronis was imprisoned for six months but eventually released on the orders of the captain of a passing French ship, who negotiated an amnesty between the squabbling colonists. The irate Pronis, however, promptly reneged on the agreement. He exiled twelve of the mutineers to Bourbon (the then un-inhabited island of Réunion) and also executed a local chief whom he believed had had an affair with his wife while he was imprisoned. His handling of the situation went from bad to worse and his final mistake was to start slave trading. A large party of Malagasy visiting the fort to trade were invited by Pronis to go along to the butcher's to find something to eat. He promptly locked them in and then handed over all seventy-three of them to a slave ship from the Dutch settlement on Mauritius. What had been a cordial relationship with the Tanosy was destroyed at a stroke.

Etienne de Flacourt was sent out to pick up the pieces, arriving in December 1648 with eighty fresh colonists and two missionaries. He got rid of Pronis at the first opportunity, putting him on a ship heading for France, and also sent Pronis's wife home to her own people. The mutineers were brought back from Réunion, possibly none too pleased to have to leave the disease-free and fertile island where they had thrived during their exile. And then, for the next five years, not one supply ship arrived. France was in the grip of civil war and the tiny colony had been all but forgotten. The colonists died one by one from fever, with occasional casualties caused by Tanosy attacks. In 1654 a French ship did finally arrive – but with no supplies. All it brought were two more missionaries and Pronis. In February 1655 Pronis became governor again when Flacourt left for home. Back in France he published two books, *Histoire de la Grande Isle Madagascar* and *Relation de la Grande Isle Madagascar*.

In 1660 Flacourt set out again from France, heading for Fort Dauphin, but he never made it. His ship was somewhere off the coast of Portugal, making for Madeira and the Canaries, when it was attacked by Barbary corsairs. These villains of the sea were pirates working out of the Barbary Coast, the North African city-states between Morocco and Egypt. Their favoured ships were long, narrow galleys powered by slave muscle. A large galley had over a hundred slaves, most of them captured Christians, shackled to their seats with four or five on each oar. Up above, these lateen-rigged ships had swivel guns along the rails and a few large cannon on the bow. Such ships were particularly effective in relatively still conditions, when they could chase and catch even the fastest quarry. Their success derived not from their cannon but from the impact of their hundred or more janissaries, soldiers who overwhelmed the opposition by leaping aboard an enemy ship after their own galley had rammed it.

By the mid-seventeenth century many of the Barbary corsairs were not Moslem 'Moors' but Europeans, either former captives converted to Islam or renegade sailors. The prize they sought was not treasure but human beings: prisoners were used as galley oarsmen or sold into slavery in North Africa and the Middle East. Wealthier captives, who had suitable connections at home, could be ransomed. Under attack from corsairs many European crews chose death rather than surrender, setting fire to their own ships' powder magazines when further resistance seemed useless. This is how Flacourt died – during the fighting the ship blew up and he and most of the crew were killed in the explosion.

Flacourt's book, though, is not his only legacy. Today the fort that the French built lies under a military barracks in Fort Dauphin. Flacourt's stone house still survives and is being turned into a museum. He even drew a detailed plan of Fort Dauphin which shows not only the fort and the houses of the colonists, but the little gardens they cultivated to survive their isolation. Today all is hidden below the houses and streets of the modern town but the buried remains are there for future archaeologists.

Although the French settlement at Fort Dauphin was tiny, the presence of the Europeans had a profound impact on southern Madagascar. They brought firearms and their soldiers clearly terrified every enemy force that they came up against. They seem to have been unstoppable, more as a result of the fear engendered by their technology and their physical appearance than for their actual military ability. The primitive matchlock muskets of the period were neither accurate nor quick to fire and their effectiveness lay mainly in the noise they made. The soldiers' red skin also gave them a major psychological advantage over their enemies and the Malagasy's fear of Europeans was exploited to the full.

Flacourt knew that he could use his small band of soldiers to considerable advantage throughout the south. He deployed them as shock troops accompanying local allies to settle scores against neighbouring kingdoms and to bring home the beef, escorting captured herds of cattle back to Fort Dauphin. His soldiers, who must have suffered in their heavy woollen clothing and metal helmets, often marched hundreds of miles right across the south and into the lands well to the north of Anosy.

They and their Malagasy scouts provided Flacourt with detailed information on the political situation and the geography of the whole region. Curiously Flacourt, living in neighbouring Anosy and talking to Tanosy informants, did not know the name 'Tandroy'. He calls them the *Ampatois*, a French formation from a Malagasy word, meaning the people of the region of 'the Ampatres'. Today we know this word as a description of the flat grassland in southern Androy. Drury, writing some seventy years later than Flacourt, never uses this term, instead calling the region 'Anterndroea'. Drury is thus the first outsider to give it an accurate name, though he uses the ethnic name Antandroy instead of the place-name Androy. Flacourt certainly knew a lot about Androy's geography and inhabitants. It had evidently always been a violent region, even before the coming of the French. The fertile river valleys had been abandoned fairly recently and the people of the Ampatres had retreated into fortified villages, far from the water sources and surrounded by defences of spiny trees.

Our exhausting weeks of survey and excavation were about to pay off. We found a site which not only gave us an insight into Flacourt's 'land of the Ampatres' but also linked it to the Tandroy world described by Robert Drury. The clue we followed lay hidden in one of Flacourt's many descriptions of the campaigns involving his troops and the local inhabitants. One place-name had survived for three-and-a-half centuries.

Flacourt had been in charge of Fort Dauphin for only six months when, in early June 1649, a delegation of Mahafaly arrived out of the west with a request from their king. He wanted the French to come and help him launch an attack on his enemy. The Mahafaly king's proposal was that they would split any booty, half for the French and half for himself. This cattle raid sounded enticing to Flacourt as it promised a fresh supply of food for the beleaguered colony, and he dispatched a party of soldiers towards the west.

On the way home from the successful raid, Flacourt's lieutenant Le Roy and the captured herd stopped in the Ampatres at a place called Montefeno, which Flacourt describes as the *grand village* of the Ampatois. This was the residence of their king, Andrianmififarivo, who received the party with full hospitality but warned them that they should trust no one, not even his own sons. Le Roy sent for reinforcements from Fort Dauphin but the messenger was murdered en route by the Ampatois. News of Le Roy's predicament did finally reach Flacourt, who sent out a rescue party.

Flacourt was a methodical, accurate reporter and his lieutenant seems to have been an observant and competent man. The mention of this royal village of Montefeno was an exciting lead for our project. Montefeno today is a big settlement in the middle of Androy's southern sandy plain. The inhabitants were very welcoming but pointed out two problems. There was no wood for cooking and no water at all. We would have to buy these in the nearby town. Preliminary inquiries about local history were not particularly productive; although people were friendly enough, nobody could think of any places to show us where they had ever noticed old pottery in the ground.

The next morning we started walking the fields. The pottery we found was just right. Being the precise sort of person that he was, Flacourt recorded for posterity the ceramic styles used in southern Madagascar in the mid-1600s. He describes a variety of cooking pots, flat dishes, sieves and deep dishes 'which they bake in a brush fire, and which become bright and shiny as if they have been varnished, after they have been rubbed with a black earth resembling antimony'. Known to archaeologists as graphite wares, these burnished pots decorated with tiny triangular designs were used only during the sixteenth and seventeenth centuries. That day we found pottery everywhere. This had plainly been a densely settled area in the last four hundred years.

At the centre of one ancient site stood a large and impressive tree. This, we were told, was a sacred tree marking the spot where the Tandroy royal family come to bury the umbilical cords of their infants. Unable to believe our luck, we listened as our guide explained the connection. Everyone knew that the royal family had once lived here, he said. This was the place of their roots, even though they had moved away long ago – to Ambaro, where we had excavated houses of the eighteenth century and where many of their descendants still live. The umbilical cords of generations of Tandroy babies confirmed a whole history. The ancient practices of the royal clan still preserve a tie with a place once inhabited by their distant ancestors, linking the written histories of Flacourt and Drury, the oral histories of the Tandroy and the dating evidence of the pottery.

The first Tandroy were a migratory people; every clan's history lists names of places successively inhabited and abandoned by their roving ancestors. In the distant past the royal clan came out of the east and moved across the south. In the mid-1600s, when Flacourt first came across the king of the Ampatres, they were living at Montefeno and the archaeology confirms settlement of that date.

Further migrations took some of the royal clan off to the west, to Ampotake on the River Manambovo, the place named in all the oral traditions as the location of the royal clan's great fission. It split into two branches when the great King Andrianjoma moved part of the clan north to Ambaro. The genealogies place King Andrianjoma in the late 1600s and the archaeology of Ambaro has confirmed settlements from then on, into the nineteenth century. Throughout all these moves and migrations, for four hundred years, the royal clan have continued to treat Montefeno as their place of origin, visiting the sacred tree to bury the umbilical cords of their babies.

We had linked seventeenth-century Montefeno to eighteenth-century Ambaro through the archaeology, Flacourt's narrative and the traditions of the royal clan. This was as close as we were going to get to proving that Ambaro was the location of the royal village inhabited in 1703, the place named as Fenoarivo by Robert Drury. King Kirindra, whom the crew of the *Degrave* met at Fenoarivo, would have been a recent successor of King Andrianmififarivo described by Flacourt as ruling at Montefeno in 1649. Drury tells us the death-names of Kirindra's own brother and father – two real jaw-breakers, Andriamangajohañarivo and Andriamaniñarivo – but we can only guess if either of these was known as Andrianmififarivo while alive.

In the twilight we returned home elated. Our evening was blighted by the discovery that the spiders sharing our house were very poisonous. Everyone peered into the nest with its spiny eggs and tutted at how dangerous these red-backs were. But nobody seemed to be terribly bothered except Karen, who abandoned etiquette and insisted on eating her dinner outside. Like the cockroaches and the fleas, spiders are merely part of the furniture which it would be too much effort or simply impolite to expend energy on killing. Anyway Georges said they were 'not exactly fatal' unless one had an allergic reaction. Our encounters with poisonous critters continued into the morning. Victor was miffed to find a scorpion in his trousers and in our tent one popped out from under a sleeping bag next to Karen's ear and had to be squashed with an archaeological trowel.

We excavated the seventeenth-century site at Montefeno with the help of crowds of small children who picked tiny morsels of pottery and charcoal from the sieved soil and identified animal bones at a glance. As we worked on our small hilltop, the valley bottom filled with another work-party: all the local inhabitants, men and women, had been called together to dig a new road. In exchange, they would receive from the World Food Programme food aid consisting of a few cups of beans and rice for each worker. As they levelled the earth road, we trowelled away to reveal the floor of an ancient house, finding pottery, beads and a piece of silver jewellery. Sometime in the 1600s this large dwelling, bigger than most Tandroy houses today, had been the home of a very wealthy family.

With the help of the children, and the interested comments of passing adults, work went well, interrupted only by a call to attend a tribunal. We had broken a taboo and had to pay a fine. One of the team (who wishes to remain anonymous) had misunderstood the directions to the village's lavatory area and one morning had chosen the wrong copse of trees. Spotted by a local man, she had been reported for violating an unmarked children's cemetery. We bought a large sheep to sacrifice and went off to a village meeting to apologise and face the music.

The sheep turned out to be a ram so before its throat was cut, the poor creature had to lose its testicles – only castrates can be sacrificed – but it went with barely a bleat of protest. We made our speeches of apology and then lost the thread of the argument going on around us. Several men in the crowd were making vehement complaints and we feared the worst. It turned out that the man who had shopped us to the authorities was himself in deep trouble: he had been illicitly collecting firewood in the cemetery forest when he spotted our team member's trip to the lavatory and was himself being fined for breaking a taboo. By that point he probably wished he'd kept his mouth shut – losing a sheep is a hefty penalty.

Headhunters and Hostages

We went to market to stock up with the usual provisions (rice, rice and yet more rice) and, to celebrate finding Montefeno, filled a bucket with delicious *habobo*, curds and whey made from sour milk fermented with tamarinds. Our jerry-cans were empty so we went off to the only water source, a deep well with steps descending about 20ft below ground. The water was mucky and pink and tasted strongly of earth. That lunchtime the rainy season began. After no water at all, there was suddenly far too much.

In spite of the weather we had to get back to work. We needed to look for the site of another ancient royal village called Anjampenorora ('At the baobab full of spit'). Georges knew roughly where it was so we set off through the rainstorm to talk to the Andriamañare, the royal clan, who lived in the area. But as we headed out to start fieldwalking, we made a serious mistake which would cause trouble later that day. Unknown to us the village where we were surveying was inhabited by two separate clans; we had introduced ourselves to only one of them and no one had thought to ask the other clan for their permission. Our day proceeded with moments of farce. It was still pouring with rain and we needed some waterproofs so Helen set to work dressing everyone up in black bin-liners. Our local guides thought we looked hilarious, like a flock of giant bats.

Small children were pointing and laughing even more than usual as we clambered through cactus hedges into the fields. By lunchtime we had found what we were looking for: handfuls of graphite-burnished pottery scattered around the margins of a sacred forest. This was what we had hoped to find: this village had been inhabited before Montefeno and we had gone even further back into the history of Androy.

We found a spot to have our picnic lunch and settled down to a real feast. We had some bread – green with mould which was sprouting at an alarming rate in the damp weather – but had forgotten to bring anything else except two cans of mixed vegetables. Jean-Luc got the tins open with a handy gadget but even he couldn't conjure up a spoon. Dressed like a group of punk rockers out of 1970s London, we sat in our bin-bags licking diced carrots off our filthy hands. Jean-Luc could take no more and collapsed in fits of giggles at the absurdity of it all.

Unfortunately not everyone could see the funny side of archaeology. As we returned to the village late that afternoon we saw waiting for us a crowd of stern-looking men. We gritted our teeth. There was going to be trouble. An elderly gent in a pink shirt launched into a lengthy condemnation of us and our unauthorised activities. Retsihisatse remained perfectly calm and answered each of his outraged accusations, explaining that we did indeed have permission but apologising for our rudeness in not knowing that we should have spoken to representatives of both clans. Fortunately an acquaintance of Retsihisatse in the crowd was brave enough to vouch for us. We meant what we said and were not headhunters.

Ramil then arrived with Helen and Jean-Luc. They decided to keep a low profile: Ramil pretended to be simple and Helen and Jean-Luc went off to entertain the children. But where was Georges? Mr Pink was very cross: a dangerous foreigner was on the loose, which seemed unwarranted given that Georges was nearly seventy, patently mild-mannered, and fluent in Tandroy. One of our guides then appeared and spoke up for us, saying that we were as good as Tandroy and squeezing our hands for support. Georges finally turned up, still wearing his bin bag and surrounded by a gaggle of children who had been keeping him company all afternoon. Their laughter and excitement finished off the encounter and we were free to go.

While we were talking to Georges and Retsihisatse about this confrontation, a couple of disturbing stories came out. There was a tale that back in 1975 the men of this village had chopped up a Catholic priest with their machetes because he had been frightening the children. In 1967 four civil servants had been murdered here, an event which Georges and Retsihisatse both recalled. Recently another civil servant had got into trouble after apparently following a woman across a field. Here was a long history of difficulties involving out-siders. But the worst was yet to come.

That evening Helen finally admitted what others had begun to suspect – she was in serious trouble with a leg injury. Exactly a month before she had cut it on sharp rocks while swimming. We had been living in far from hygienic conditions with people who suffer from endemic skin complaints, including yaws, a highly contagious disease related to syphilis. Antibiotic powder was no longer working and the wound was now horribly infected. Her leg was very swollen and as hard as a brick but she had simply not wanted to bother the rest of us with it. The next morning Victor drove her to the town of Ambovombe where there would be a doctor. Helen was unfortunately the only member of the party who couldn't speak French so Jean-Luc went with her as interpreter and moral support. On the way they dropped off the rest of us to continue fieldwalking not far from Montefeno.

In the village where we hoped to survey that day, the women were stringing up cotton thread dyed brown and yellow, to be woven into the distinctive funeral *lamba* with which the Tandroy adorn a coffin for its journey to the tomb. Someone produced a beautiful finished *lamba* of yellow stripes on a dark brown background, with small lead beads threaded into the pattern at its ends. They claimed it was woven from silk – coarse raw silk was used in the last century and is now enjoying a small revival. Did we want to buy it? Retsihisatse was suspicious. He had worked with the anthropologist Sarah Fee, whose specialism was textiles, and thought these weavers were asking far too much. In fact the women knew Sarah because she had done some of her research in the village next door. They seemed perfectly relaxed about our presence and offered to look after our lunch bag while we went fieldwalking.

We were engrossed in pottery on a large settlement site when we noticed a deputation of about thirty men on the horizon, definitely coming our way. They were armed with spears, slings, axes and very large machetes. We decided to sit down and wait. When they reached us the shouting started. The spokesman's main complaint was that we were frightening the children, although the fifteen or so youngsters tagging along seemed to think this was terribly funny, as they sniggered throughout. The arguments gradually petered out and the men stomped off, back towards the village. We followed, to retrieve our lunch and to try to put things right.

Sitting in a little house which one of the women offered us as a dining room, Ramil produced the official paperwork. We had often shown our papers to soldiers and policemen at the many armed checkpoints on major roads and also to regional civil servants but never like this, in a little village. Producing such a stack of permits would normally be rather intimidating so this was a last resort. Many of the men were still very agitated. We had not resolved the situation.

Ramil and Retsihisatse postponed further discussion – they were hungry and wanted to tuck into our packed lunch which had been augmented by some sweet potatoes brought by our hostess. It is terribly impolite to watch other people eating and everyone withdrew to leave us in peace. Ominously, they also closed the door, shutting us in.

We were getting worried and had entirely lost our appetites, while Ramil and Retsihisatse were eating as much as they could. Their explanation was that we might need our strength if things took a turn for the worse. Looking around in the gloom of the house, we spotted a spear propped in a corner and an axe. We could always go down fighting if it came to it. Retsihisatse was optimistic. The deputation had come out to find us with their spears pointing upwards, he explained. Had they carried them with the tips pointing down then we would really have been in trouble.

After lunch a large group of men gathered outside the house. We had to stay indoors, shut in with a noisy chicken, while Ramil and Retsihisatse presented our case. There were mutterings about our paperwork. Our papers clearly stated that we had permission to work in Madagascar – but not in Androy, said one man, clearly unable to read that Androy and Mahafaly are specified in our permits as the only parts of Madagascar that we *do* have authorisation for. 'Is Androy part of Madagascar anyway?' asked another. Evidently no one could read. How could we prove we weren't headhunters?

The president of the area was sent for and he finally arrived to chair the meeting. We sat in the house, peering through a crack and listening to the talking. People repeated that the children were terribly frightened. Even the women were said to have been afraid, although they had actually only been interested in trying to flog us an over-priced *lamba*. This is a claim we have heard again and again in other parts of Androy. None of the men is ever afraid of anything, of course, but foreigners might frighten the women and children. And yet it is very clear that the men are scared to the point of paranoia.

Once again, just as the day before, we learnt that earlier incidents triggered this fear and hostility. The leader of the deputation which found us in the fields told the assembly that he once saw a foreigner and four Malagasy stopping near him in a car. The Malagasy got out, he says; they were obviously being sent to attack him so he ran away. Other people described an incident in which a foreigner came by in a car. He stopped, which alarmed people, so they had tried to barricade him in with roadblocks of fallen trees. This wicked foreigner had looked very cross and had then driven off without any explanations, confirming people's ideas of his evil intentions. We had a sneaking suspicion that behind both these horror stories about thwarted headhunters were some lost travellers trying to ask for directions . . . .

Around a quarter past three the mood finally changed. The grim voices were interrupted by the sound of occasional laughter in the crowd and soothing words from the president. Our brief experience of being held hostage was over and we were free to go. We asked for a guide to come with us for what was left of the afternoon but still no one fancied the job.

We set off anyway, with the village's blessing, to find more sites and along the way picked up two boys who willingly agreed to act as guides. That evening we arrived back in the village to smiling faces, except for that of the boys' distraught mother. They had stayed out later than they were allowed, as boys will, and she was worrying that maybe we were headhunters after all. It was getting dark by the time Victor finally turned up in the Landrover, without either Helen or Jean-Luc.

A note from them explained that they had found a doctor, who had realised immediately that Helen's leg was in a desperately serious condition. The infection was near the bone and another day or so later and her leg may have been beyond saving. The doctor had started her on massive doses of antibiotics but she wasn't out of the woods yet. Jean-Luc and Helen would be staying in town until things improved.

The next morning Retsihisatse found the largest and nastiest-looking knife we owned and strapped it to his belt. In the last forty-eight hours he had been through two lengthy episodes of anger and intimidation. As a Tandroy he had borne the brunt of most of the harangues and questioning and, like the rest of us, was feeling ground down and twitchy. Our survey plan was to complete a long transect through the landscape but we were going to have to leave a small gap. Causing more distress to the unfriendly inhabitants was not worth it – we were certainly not going back to finish that patch.

As it turned out, the next two days were free of hassle. The weather was perfect and we were working in a delightful landscape of rolling hills and little woods. The villagers we met were perfectly happy to show us around and in one village we bought three turkeys (*vorom'tsy loza* or 'the not-dangerous bird' in Tandroy!), one to share as a farewell meal with our hosts and one each for Ramil and Victor to take home to Tana. That evening, after Victor had beheaded our dinner, we sat down to a turkey feast and plenty of home-made rum.

In Ambovombe we found Jean-Luc and Helen and heard the grisly story of her leg. In his surgery, a little wooden shack without electricity or running water, the doctor had given her huge injections of penicillin. He had reamed quantities of pus out of the deep hole in her leg, every day unplugging and refilling the cavity with yards of gauze. There was no anaesthetic – Helen remembers banging her head on the surgery table to distract herself from the pain – but she was now recovering.

Installed in our favourite *hotely*, we drink cold beer and realise that our work for the season has almost come to an end. We can try to forget the upsetting near-disasters of the last few days. Helen, although wobbly, is on the mend and even manages a smile at the old joke: 'What's yaws?' 'Mine's a pint.' There are baskets of pottery filling the Landrover, a crate of turkeys on the roof-rack and we will all be home for Christmas. The nervous tension evaporates and Ramil is soon fast asleep at the lunch table.

Guns and Battles

Our brief experience of being held hostage is the only encounter with anything approaching violence that we have ever had with the Tandroy. Warfare and armed cattle raiding were common in the past, but both have been long suppressed by the state authorities. Although Tandroy men still carry spears, we have only seen them used to puncture the throats of sacrificial steers at funerals. We have never even seen a fist-fight, despite the heavy drinking and courting of girls indulged in by crowds of young men during the heightened atmosphere of a funeral.

Among Madagascar's natural resources are seams of precious stones and a recent sapphire boom has brought guns and the threat of violence to this remarkably peaceful society. On one of the major roads across the south, near a national park, a Wild West town has grown from nowhere. Across the country schools have emptied as even teachers and pupils join the flood of young men heading to the sapphire mines to seek their fortune. Tandroy villages often seem deserted: no one is left except a few women and children since the men have all gone to the mines. Some die in the unpropped mine tunnels and the lucky few who find instant wealth are vulnerable to murderous attack. Armed checkpoints on the roads attempt to catch the foreign dealers who have arrived in the country illegally to trade for the stones. The sieves and shovels on our Landrover's roof-rack raise many suspicions – now we are suspected of being both headhunters and sapphire miners. Violence is in the air and guns are back in the south.

Drury's experience of violence was very different, and on our next expedition we set off to follow the course of the battles in which he fought. We got off to a slow start. We tried cabling money in advance to Ramil so that he could get the Landrover mended before our arrival, but the university finance department was being unusually difficult and we had trouble persuading them that Ramilisonina, a man with only one name, really existed. The money was late arriving in Madagascar and when we arrived the repairs had not been done.

The Landrover had been diagnosed as needing major repairs and the Musée had somehow been inveigled into taking it into a military garage in Antananarivo. Our colleagues were reluctant to comment on what might be going on and it took us a while to realise that oblique hints were being dropped that all was not well. We decided to abandon tact and delicacy and staked out the garage at dawn. There the Landrover lay, with its guts all over the floor. We could tell from the thick coating of dust that nothing had been done to it for many weeks. Victor had a good look and a Good Look (a brand of Malagasy cigarette). It was serious. We would need to find even more money to buy parts and he reckoned that the repairs might take several weeks.

We had to hire another vehicle already in working order. The team split up into several hunting parties and soon learnt that the flashy four-wheel-drives sometimes available from tour companies were way beyond our budget and anyway far too small given the amount of equipment and food we had to carry. Our prospects were looking grim until Victor spotted a blue long-wheelbase Landrover near his house and discovered that it was for hire.

A couple of days later we had filled in all our paperwork, including a cast-iron contract with the Malagasy man named John who was the vehicle's chauffeur – as with all hired cars in Madagascar, the driver had to come too. We were not going to leave Victor behind though, so all seven of us squeezed in and off we went to meet up with Georges and Retsihisatse. We were already late and delays soon mounted. By the second day the roof-rack was coming adrift but, after a spot of welding, we continued gingerly on our way. John had never been to the south before and was perturbed to hear that we would be stopping for the night in Ambalavao.

Ambalavao is the most beautiful town in Madagascar, at the heart of its wine-growing region. The town straddles the two cultures of Madagascar: it is on the edge of the rice-growing zone and also the location of the big cattle market to which the pastoralists of the south walk their herds to sell to the people of the highlands. Whenever we drive back from Androy it is always the point at which we can reckon to have left the dry and uncompromising landscape of the south. We were looking forward to staying at the traditional paper-making centre which has lovely guestrooms, but for John the town was a place of terror. Ambalavao is notorious throughout Madagascar for its *pamosavy*: witches who steal your soul in the night. We suspected that if John thought Ambalavao was bad, he was not going to enjoy Androy very much.

In the morning everyone had slept well except John, who reckoned that someone had been in his room, tugged at his bedding and stolen a tee-shirt. The following night we crept into Beraketa, the town which just about marks the northern limit of Androy today. The roof-rack had disintegrated completely.

By the time we reached Androy Georges and his family were on the point of leaving for Fort Dauphin, but Retsihisatse was ready to come with us. We headed down to the mouth of the River Manambovo but fieldwalking became a stressful nightmare. People were very anxious about 'red foreigner' headhunters. We made ever greater efforts to notify all the different authorities of our presence and spent hours in each village explaining ourselves and discussing what we were doing there. At every meeting it was clear that many of the men were very frightened. The old ladies, though, would push their way to the front and have a good stare at us, apparently not the least bit worried.

We had good, bad and surreal moments. The good moments were when we met people who were genuinely interested in finding out about their ancient places. Théophile was a fisherman who had travelled widely. He was not only delightful company but also a mine of information about the ancient sites and pottery scatters in the area around his village. Ever conscious of how easily people could be frightened by us, we made painfully slow progress. Parts of the landscape in which we worked with Théophile as our guide were a lunar wasteland of giant dunes and rolling sands, miles inland from the sea. One of our most intriguing finds was the remains of a village first settled around Drury's time and occupied through to the nineteenth century. It had then been buried under an enormous sand dune and was only now being exposed by the wind.

The most peculiar incident came when listening to Jean-Luc's little radio one morning. A French international station was describing a car accident in Paris the night before. We soon discovered we were living in one of the many places in the world where no one had heard of Diana, Princess of Wales, or cared much about how she died. Far more important to our colleagues and the villagers was news of a football match: Madagascar had defeated Canada in the Francophone Nations' Games.

We were not sorry to finish the survey and go. Nothing was working out smoothly this field season. We stopped in the local market to buy provisions and say farewell and Jean-Luc endured hours of being hectored by a drunken old man whose insults washed over him along with the spittle, much to the amusement of other market-goers. Our colleagues shook their heads and flatly refused to translate what was being said.

By the time we got on our way it was already afternoon. We were heading eastwards down the coast, hoping, just hoping, that we might be able to go right back to the beginning of Robert Drury's story – to the shipwreck itself. We had come across a tiny footnote in a book from 1912. The French administrator Emile Defoort had once seen and measured two iron cannon, one on a reef and the other on a sandy beach, on the coast somewhere south of Ambovombe. Relocating two cannon buried somewhere on the miles of Androy seashore was always going to be a long shot, and given our luck so far our expectations were very low, but it all proved remarkably straightforward.

During the years we had been investigating Drury's story Mike had been working over topographical descriptions and other clues in *Robert Drury's Journal* to pinpoint the most likely site of the *Degrave*'s landfall on the shores of Androy. Adding in Defoort's location, we knew where we wanted to start looking, so we called in at the nearest small town. There was a local council meeting in session, luckily nearly finished, so we waited and then explained our quest. To our astonishment the councillors knew all about these cannon and one of them, a lobster diver, suggested that if we gave him a lift home he could take us there immediately.

With the sun going down we parked on top of the high sand cliff and ran as fast as we could down the steep path to the beach. There, simply lying on the reef, was an 8ft long cannon, the incoming tide washing over it. We all ran into the water and danced around it in our excitement. None of us knew much about dating cannon but Defoort had been certain that those he had seen were from the *Degrave* and this one looked about right. The councillor-fisherman explained that there was another big iron object buried under the sand about 300 yards away. We would wait for low tide and dig it out, making copious notes and drawings and taking photographs so that the specialists back in Britain would be able to identify and date the guns.

That evening we set up home in the councillor's village. He told us that a man from a museum had been here two years before and had watched from the shore while local snorkel divers had swum out through the dangerous surf to tell him what lay beyond the reef and to bring up any manageable finds. We realised that we were on the tracks of a colleague. We knew that a naval officer seconded to the Musée had investigated a potential wreck site somewhere in Androy, but from his description of the site's location he seemed to have been talking about a completely different area and a different wreck. But the locals insisted that this was the site that he had visited and claimed to have dived on.

The captain had supervised the recovery of part of a bronze ship's bell, initially burying it in the sand for safety and then, sadly, breaking it into pieces for easy transport. During our prolonged delay in Antananarivo we had drawn and photographed fragments of this bell. The captain's description of the cannon he had seen had sounded like a hoop-and-stave gun of the sixteenth century – which these cannon definitely weren't. To confuse matters further, he had told the locals that it was the site of an Arab shipwreck. As we talked around the camp fire with the councillor we learnt that there were no stories about the wreck, but there was more tangible information. Another four cannon and an anchor lay on the sea bed at a depth of 2.5 metres in the turbulent waters immediately beyond the reef.

The next day a crowd accompanied us to the beach. None of us felt brave enough to go snorkelling on the wreck site – there are sharks out there – but a couple of lobster fishermen were swimming through the surf, even though it looked as if it might pound them against the reef at any moment. The men told us that the second cannon was buried some way down the beach from the first, and after a bit of judicious probing with a spade we soon found it and dug away the sand. It was very similar to the cannon resting on the reef and we settled down to draw both guns and survey accurate positions for them.

There was nothing that we could actually do with the cannon other than record them, and by lunchtime we had finished. We arranged to return the following season to meet the divers again, to get more information on the cannon out on the reef, but this return trip went badly. The local mayor attempted to extort money from Ramil, who found himself trying to explain not only the details of our project but also the duties of a Malagasy civil servant, the concept of a museum and the legal powers of a town council! When this tiresome meeting finally concluded, all the divers turned out to be blind drunk and the weather was far too dangerous to permit diving anyway. The cannon have been identified as Swedish 'finbankers', a type of gun commonly used on East India Company ships in the early eighteenth century. The shipwreck is the right date for the *Degrave* and no others of the period are recorded for this coastline. The remains are still out there on the reef.

After our first reconnaissance of the cannon, we headed off in search of rest and relaxation at the nature reserve of Berenty. Just west of the Mandrare, this tourist haven is technically in Androy but is a little woodland paradise, insulated from the world outside. There are chalets with beds, showers and real toilets. The resident ring-tailed lemurs are accustomed to people and utterly delightful, bold enough to walk into the chalets carrying their babies on their backs. Our short period of field survey in Berenty was luxurious. By day we strolled around the shady estate looking for sherds and by night we drank in the bar and ate in the restaurant. Here we met Alison Jolly, an American lemur expert who is also a great fan of Drury's. She was very excited by our findings and we talked for hours about cannon and kings. We would happily have stayed longer in Berenty to watch Alison's students watching the lemurs, but the team was going soft and our field schedule was far from over. We set off again, westwards towards Mahafaly country. Feeling pretty confident after our first attempt at semi-underwater archaeology, we were now going to try some battlefield archaeology.

When Robert Drury finally made his break for freedom in about 1710 or 1711, he was heading for trouble. One morning he slipped out of Miavaro's village at dawn and ran. The mountain of Angavo was the first stop on his escape route to the west. The distance he covered was normally a two-day walk but he reached Angavo by nightfall and thought he had made almost 60 miles in a day. Throughout his book Drury consistently overestimates distances – in fact he had come less than 25 miles. Still, he had escaped the clutches of the

horrible Miavaro and was greeted cordially by the brother of
the rebel prince Mananjaka, whom he had met during his brief
stay in Angavo's mountain-top village during the civil war.
Drury was presented with a gun, a sign that he was no longer a
slave, although he was not going to be allowed to leave. He
spent the next six months hunting wild cattle and spying out
the lie of the land.

Drury still had an escape route in his head, gleaned from a
conversation with the ambassador from the Fiherenana
kingdom on the west coast. He had to head north from Angavo
and then strike out to the north-west. He would pass through
the territories of three kings, the last of whom lived at the head
of the River Onilahy which flows into St Augustine's Bay, his
final destination. It would mean a hard journey, on foot and
alone, and might take as long as six weeks.

But before he was able to get away, Drury had to go to war
once more. The ambassador from the west arrived in Androy
for a second time, to announce that the Fiherenana army was
on the march against the Mahafaly and their king. The conflict
between the Mahafaly and their neighbours to the north had
come to a head over a dog: the Mahafaly king had given his
hound the same name as the king of the Fiherenana, an
unforgivable insult. The ambassador had come to Angavo to
call the Tandroy to join a new attack on the Mahafaly.

With this allied army of six thousand men Drury marched to
the borders of Mahafaly country. On reaching the River
Menarandra, the frontier, they found that the villages along it
had been abandoned, probably about a fortnight earlier. They
peered across the river at King Hosintany's capital on the
further bank and saw that it too was empty. The army crossed
the river into Mahafaly territory and set up camp on a plain on
its west bank. This was where they would fight the enemy. In
preparation for the coming engagement the invaders
constructed a circular fort from felled trees and earth scooped
up from a shallow trench around the outside, making a solid
wall about 4ft high with two narrow entrances. At dawn the
Mahafaly attacked but were beaten off and routed. As far as

Drury could tell the soldiers on both sides were off their heads, having smoked large amounts of cannabis to brace themselves for the fighting.

The allies marched further into Mahafaly country, destroying crops and plundering villages. Drury was attached to a battalion which headed south, reaching the sea after a day and a moonlit night's march. They were following the tracks of a large herd of cattle which had been driven along the beach in an attempt to hide the animals' hoofprints in the tide, and had then been led inland. As ever, the main aim of the invasion was to seize as much wealth as possible, in the form of slaves and the enemy's cattle herds. Drury's force had a successful mission. After walking all day they found and captured the Mahafaly cattle herd, with only one man lost. This poor fellow was bending over to wash his *lamba* when he was killed 'by a random Shot, which he receiv'd in his Posteriors'. Back at the camp the captured cattle were shared out between the allies. The entire army marched back to Angavo and the warriors of the Fiherenana then left for home.

Drury had now twice had contact with the people of the west. He knew for certain that English ships did pass there – some of the Fiherenana men had even spoken a few words of English, although it was so long since Drury had heard his native language that he had only been able to reply in Malagasy. He was determined to follow them to the west and the possibility of rescue at St Augustine. Back on Angavo, he was kept under guard for two months until the grass had grown over the Fiherenana army's homeward route but eventually, during a hunting expedition, he seized an opportunity to slip away into the night.

Escape

Drury's journey to freedom took twenty-seven days. One night he was attacked by wild animals and bitten in the foot and face by a 'fox', probably the creature called a *fossa*. The *fossa* is not a large animal and seems very shy of people, but the forest people of the south-west still fear the bites inflicted by this animal. An infection set in to the wounds and Drury had to hole up for days, waiting for his foot to recover.

When he set off again, he laboured through hills until, on the seventeenth day after leaving Angavo, he reached flat plains and the Onilahy river. Arriving in the Fiherenana, ten days later, Drury sought refuge in the village of one of the princes whom he had met during the campaigns and waited in vain for a ship to arrive at the port of St Augustine. He did start to pick up his lost mother tongue again because here in the Fiherenana lived a West Indian and a West African dumped there years before by pirates. Both men and their children spoke English, which Drury at first struggled to understand.

War was still in the air and in about 1712, a year or more after Drury's arrival in the west, a fresh invasion was mounted into Mahafaly country. This time Drury was in the Fiherenana arm of the allied army and was sent to march in front of the troops, carrying a sacred battle talisman. When his army joined their Tandroy allies, Drury had to face his old master Miavaro again, whom he fobbed off with false promises that he would go back to Androy after the battle was over. At the end of the successful campaign Drury was given a prisoner of war to be his slave. Along with the five cattle which he was awarded, Drury was also offered a slave girl, but 'as I had already a Man, who was as much as I wanted, I desir'd to have two Cows instead'. Drury now had economic security and a slave with the resonant name of Sambo. As odd as it may sound to our ears, the word actually means 'ship' and is still a common boys' name in the south.

Drury's former masters among the Tandroy suffered badly in the aftermath of the war. The warriors of the Mahafaly king shadowed the Tandroy army home and made a final night-time attack, killing King Kirindra himself and many of his men. Kirindra's son then failed in a bid to succeed his father and fled to Anosy. Prince Mananjaka was proclaimed the new *roandria* or king of Androy.

Our team was off into the unknown, into the land of the Mahafaly on the trail of the armies with whom Drury twice marched into enemy territory in about 1710 and 1712. We wanted to find the Mahafaly capital of King Hosintany. Might we also be able to find the earthworks of the fortified camps erected by the Tandroy–Fiherenana forces?

We had roughed out the first area to survey, along the Menarandra river, led by Drury's account, existing place-names and earlier archaeological exploration. In the 1980s Chantal Radimilahy, one of the Musée's senior researchers, had surveyed the site of a royal capital founded by Hosintany's eldest son Tsimamandy, a great king whose deeds are still related in many tales. She found the remains of a settlement occupied from the mid-eighteenth until the mid-nineteenth century when it was abandoned by Tsimamandy's successors who moved the capital downriver. We surmised that the earlier capital of Hosintany would lie a little further upstream, perhaps near the villages of Andriamanda ('Royal enclosure') and another Fenoarivo ('Full of a thousand').

We crossed the Manambovo over the pot-holed bridge at Tsiombe and headed west, following the route of a pipeline being put in by a Japanese aid agency to bring water from the Menarandra to the market town of Beloha. The town was without electricity but maybe soon it would have running water. Startled by the incongruity of the high-tech equipment within the low-tech setting, we looked enviously at the heavy digging machinery and thought how we could do with borrowing some of it. The filled-in channels at the mouth of the Manambovo which we had examined while looking for remains of the Elephant Bird might yield a lot more information if we could only get deep into the ancient sediments to sample them – a forlorn hope without major equipment.

Across the Menarandra the map was unusually incomplete and we were well outside Retsihisatse's country. We were soon lost on the tracks through the unknown woods when we chanced upon a hamlet hidden in dense forest. The villagers seemed to see us as a good source of entertainment and invited us to stay. We could be teased and laughed at to make the evening a little more fun. Although we thought we were already in Mahafaly country, these villagers said they were Tandroy, migrants from the Manambovo estuary. Retsihisatse was relieved: the last war between the Tandroy and the Mahafaly was in 1932 but relations are still stilted and uneasy. When we did stay at a Mahafaly village on a subsequent expedition to the coast, Retsihisatse and the local men initially treated each other very guardedly. After suspicions were allayed, Retsihisatse and the oldest Mahafaly man indicated the relaxing of tension by spending the rest of the day walking hand-in-hand, a signal of male friendship which both Mike and Jean-Luc find hugely uncomfortable since it is so alien to our own culture.

The villagers in the forests of the Menarandra told us that the Mahafaly had moved out of this riverside region years ago and there was no one left who knew about the ancient places here. Although this was now their home, the incomers had a vaguer idea than we did about the region's ancient history. However, they would come with us in the next couple of days to show us around and, more importantly, to stop others from being frightened.

The name Andriamanda turned out to belong to a clump of tamarind trees, where we soon found pottery. This had been a big village, almost identical in date to the eighteenth-century village which we had located back in Androy at Ambaro, our best candidate for the Tandroy royal village. We were looking at a plausible location for Hosintany's capital. Unprompted, our guides told us that to the south of where we were field-walking was a flat, open plain, covering 4 square kilometres. It was called Ny Alia – 'the battle'. This was known as the ancient site where the Mahafaly met attacking forces. The way they talked about it, it sounded like a martial version of a football pitch. Here was the home team's ground where battles should be fought. Could this have been the plain mentioned by Drury in both campaigns? From his description we were certainly in the right area. The ancient battlefield was as flat as a pancake, but we searched for the slightest humps and bumps that might have been left from the digging of a circular ditch 1ft deep and 7ft wide three hundred years ago. But, as we really expected, there was nothing. Such insubstantial earthworks would have been filled in and rendered invisible after a few heavy rains.

At the spot marked on the map as Fenoarivo we found a second early eighteenth-century settlement. Which one might have been the village seen by Drury? We plumped for Fenoarivo since it occupied a commanding position, perched above the riverbed on a 5m-high sand cliff and clearly visible from the east bank, as Drury states, whereas the other would have been hidden in forest.

It was now late afternoon and we had a very long hike back to the Landrover. On the way home we had to negotiate the confluence of the Menarandra and a major tributary and we had a hunch we might find an early *manda* at the spot where the two rivers met. Our surveys of the prehistoric stone enclosures on Androy's other major river, the Manambovo, indicated that these river junctions were prime locations for such sites. As we reached the junction of the two watercourses (both bone dry at this season) we looked up at the great cliff where the two rivers joined. It was stunning, about 100ft high and sheer. Perched high above the river, overlooking the surrounding area, this would be an ideal spot for a settlement. Running and scrambling, we panted along the bed of the tributary towards the setting sun until we reached a place where we could clamber up the bank beyond the great cliff. Up on top the level ground surface was oozing pottery sherds.

The clifftop was eroding fast and a small piece of ground detached itself even while we were there, warning us not to go too close to the edge. We started picking up pottery, all of it in the highly distinctive style of the fourteenth and fifteenth centuries. There were even pieces of Chinese celadon that someone must have brought upriver from coastal traders more than six hundred years ago. This was a marvellous site, but night was falling and we had to be gone.

When we finally located the Landrover in pitch darkness, Victor had almost given us up for lost. That night we decided to celebrate and drove around the forest in search of some good rum. Yes, someone had some that we could buy but no, it wasn't any good. We bought it anyway but it was seriously undrinkable and back in our hosts' village we forced down only a few mouthfuls before regretfully tipping the rest away.

We had made some intriguing discoveries which supported Drury's story, and on our second expedition to Mahafaly country we found sites of even earlier periods. On the windswept coast we excavated an ancient site of the eleventh century and also found evidence of settlers arriving from mainland Africa. The culture of the Swahili coast of East Africa used distinctive pottery, quite unlike anything of Malagasy manufacture, and we were delighted to discover Swahili pottery in the remains of a settlement in the far south-west. This was evidence that, long ago in Madagascar's past, people sailed here directly from the African coast.

In contrast to Androy, we found no sign of settlements in Mahafaly dating to the 1600s. Re-reading the French governor Flacourt's account of the Mahafaly, written in 1658, we found information which explained the absence of any villages from this period:

The country of the Mahafaly is full of woods, the inhabitants do not cultivate the ground at all . . . *They have no villages or fixed living places: for they move about as pastures become exhausted* in an area extending 35 to 40 leagues in which they can encamp. They make their huts or cabins in the woods, distant one from another, following the pens in which they keep their livestock. [Our italics.]

Flacourt found the Mahafaly nomadic lifestyle sufficiently different from that of the Tandroy and the Tanosy to comment on in some detail and this history of highly transitory settlement explains why we found no great villages from that period.

Our work in Mahafaly country was over for the year. One moonlit night we finally rolled into Retsihisatse's home village at two o'clock in the morning having traversed some truly terrible roads. The petrol was sufficient, the roof-rack held and we eventually made it back to Tana without further major breakdowns, having been entertained at one of our stops en route by a convent of very elderly Italian nuns having a party.

Cave ab Incolis
(Watch out for the Locals)

The hunt for Robert Drury is really a footnote to the major part of our fieldwork in Madagascar. Our Anglo-Malagasy team is concerned with investigating the history of Madagascar, not the story of one obscure Englishman. Drury's adventures may not be the story of a great man whose actions influenced the course of history, but it is a valuable text for Madagascar and its people. Its worth lies in its recording of Tandroy life in the eighteenth century, a period beyond the reach of oral traditions, which contributes to our research on settlement histories and the development of the monumental tombs of the south.

Drury's book is also a record of one incident of culture contact, a by-way in the history of colonialism. The meeting of Europe and the world beyond its shores has left a legacy which affects all of us today. The experience of colonialism is, however, very different from country to country, at both ends of the relationship. France's relations with her former colonies are rather different from those of Britain and the Common-wealth. Our pursuit of Drury's story has been a hunt for traces of a single encounter between the Tandroy and the outside world, an encounter which exemplifies the violence recorded in all the accounts of early contact between the people of southern Madagascar and the explorers and traders of Europe.

The arrival of Europeans in the far south from the sixteenth to the late nineteenth century had effects unlike anything experienced elsewhere in the world. Yes, there was slaving and piracy, disease and colonial settlement, but the forms that these took were unique. In Madagascar it was the Europeans who died of disease. The colonial settlements were a complete failure. The desire of the European visitors to buy human beings was no great surprise since slavery was a part of life for the indigenous people. More importantly, the people of southern Madagascar were never particularly interested in any trade goods other than guns, so the slave trade with the outside world was on a small scale and the locals resisted all attempts at colonisation by incomers.

The European explorers of the Indian Ocean arrived sixty-five years after the last Chinese expeditions of the fifteenth century. The Portuguese first sighted the island of Madagascar in 1500, naming it São Lourenço – Ile St Laurent to the French and St Lawrence's Island to the English. The Tandroy first saw European ships in 1506 when Portuguese explorers sailed along Madagascar's south coast. In 1527 came the earliest known European shipwreck: six hundred men came ashore from two Portuguese vessels somewhere on the south-west coast, probably in Mahafaly. Only about seventy of them escaped death at the hands of the locals. These survivors walked as far as Ranofotsy Bay in Anosy where they met up with other shipwrecked Portuguese and a marooned sailor from a French ship. A stone fort near Fort Dauphin called the Trañovato ('stone house') has been excavated by Georges Heurtebize and Pierre Vérin; this fort may have been built by these Portuguese sailors or may have already been there when they arrived. Whichever, it didn't offer them much in the way of defence because the Tanosy attacked and killed all but five of them. These lucky souls were taken off in 1531 by a passing ship.

French explorers followed the route opened by the great Portuguese navigators and occasionally ships would stop at Madagascar to search for supplies. It was a risky undertaking and the shore parties did not always get away unscathed. The first British citizen ever to set foot on the island died of spear wounds on his second day ashore. The south coast of Madagascar became known as a place to be avoided and in

1547 Jean Fonteneau wrote: 'The people there are negroes and valiant: but they are wicked and do not wish to trade merchandise with any strangers.'

The next wave of Europeans trying their luck in southern Madagascar came from the Netherlands. In 1595 Cornelius van Houtman's Java fleet reached Madagascar and sent a ship's launch to land at Cap Sainte Marie, its most southerly point. They encountered local people and the meeting seems to have passed off peacefully. Later Houtman's crew anchored at Fenambosy (or Ampalaza, 'the place of masts', once called St John's Bay) at the Menarandra's mouth. They learned little about the inhabitants except that the people were ruled by a chief called a *roandria* and they soon walked themselves into an ambush from which they escaped by firing a single shot. They sailed off westwards and landed again at St Augustine.

Here two of the crew were sent ashore to go and find provisions. Since these two sailors were men who had been accused of mutiny, it sounds as if there were no volunteers for the job! Ominously, the two men never returned but the local inhabitants did later make contact with the ship. Houtman recorded that they were interested in the crew's pewter spoons and offered a ten-year-old girl in exchange for one. Yet communications soon broke down and Houtman lost 122 of his crew here, either dead from disease or killed by the locals. His savage reprisals soured future relationships. When he returned to St Augustine in 1599 everyone had run away and after five weeks the sailors were able to buy only a single cow and some milk. In Houtman's opinion, Madagascar was *Coemiterium Batavorum*, the cemetery of the Dutch.

An Englishman, John Davis, had been on Houtman's second voyage and he came back as chief pilot on the English East India Company's first voyage to Madagascar in 1601, calling at the Bay of Antongil in north-east Madagascar. With the beginning of English interest in the island, an East India Company fleet reached St Augustine's Bay in 1607 and relations between the English and the people of the Fiherenana were gradually built up, remedying Houtman's disastrous encounter and establishing St Augustine as a stopping-off point for the Indies.

It was still an unpredictable spot. One ship which stopped there in 1609 after becoming separated from the rest of the East India fleet lost two crewmen murdered by the locals and one merchant taken captive, but by 1638 the situation on the west coast seems to have improved for the Europeans. Trade was flourishing and ships could expect to exchange silver coins and red cornelian beads for cattle, and brass wire for sheep, chickens, fish, milk and oranges.

In March 1645 three shiploads of English settlers landed at St Augustine. They had been taken in by advertising. Two pamphlets, *Madagascar, the Richest and most fruitful island in the World* and *A Paradox proving that the inhabitants of the isle called Madagascar or St Laurence (in Temporall things) are the happiest People in the World*, had been written by a surgeon named Walter Hamond after a visit to St Augustine in 1630 and promised a land free of sickness and a paradise on earth. About 140 people fell for this bizarre piece of propaganda and sailed for Madagascar.

On arrival these colonists were dismayed by the arid climate and harsh landscape and discovered that they had not brought with them the crucial item that they would need if they were to survive – red trade beads. Furthermore, their timing was hopeless. They arrived at the end of the rainy season so had nothing to do except watch their crops die and their cattle starve on the withering pasture. By August many had died from dysentery and fever. Their commander, John Smart, was a dangerous liability, recording in a letter that most of his male colonists were 'old, ignorant, weak fellowes' and that the women colonists were 'she-cattle [of] no other use but to destroy victuals'. Smart then made a fatal error which was to cost the lives of most of the colonists and the future of the colony.

The local *roandria* offered to supply the settlers with cattle if their forty armed men would help him fight against another clan. Smart was not taken with the proposition because previous support had not produced the promised cattle and, besides, the *roandria*'s men had been stealing the colonists' animals. He sent his men to meet the *roandria* whom the colonists then abducted and ransomed back to his people for two hundred head of cattle. Relations with the inhabitants never recovered.

During the next rainy season another thirty-seven settlers died from disease and attack. They were living on starvation rations, but Smart tried to make the best of it, writing that cattle hide was 'very good meat if well dress'd'. The colony survived for barely a year. In May 1646 the few survivors were taken off by two ships; before leaving they burned all their houses and buried letters warning others of what had befallen them in such a dreadful spot.

It didn't seem so terrible when we visited St Augustine recently: the beautiful bay of blue water, seafood bought from the local fishermen and stunning views from the surrounding mountains all seemed idyllic. The little town which now lies at the mouth of the Onilahy river may sit on top of the failed English settlement, or its remains may have been lost to the river. Unlike the sand-rivers of Androy, the Onilahy flows with water and in its lowest reaches has changed course several times. The last remains of the dead English immigrants have probably been taken by the sea.

If the situation in St Augustine was bad in the 1600s, the deep south was even worse. Only the misfortune of shipwreck took anyone there. Flacourt wrote about two Dutch wrecks, one around 1618 and the other about twenty years later. The first left only one survivor, the captain's son Pitre, who washed up on the Karembola shore. He narrowly escaped death and then lived with the locals for two years and learned Malagasy. One of the Tanosy *roandria* heard about him and brought him to Anosy, setting him up with a house, a wife and slaves. Pitre lived with the Tanosy for a further five years until picked up by a Dutch ship.

In about 1636 another ship sank about 3 or 4 leagues (9–12 miles) west of the Manambovo. The five hundred men who reached shore built themselves a boat and a wooden fort. At first they traded for cattle with the inhabitants but the locals kept stealing them back. The situation escalated into violence and several Europeans, including the captain, were killed. The officers and some hundred men sailed off in the boat, leaving the rest to their fate. Many died of disease and the survivors eventually wandered off in search of rescue.

Their ship had been laden with a large amount of silver and the men setting out from the wooden fort each carried two or three hundred pieces-of-eight. They were ambushed and killed in Androy for their clothes and silver and only two of them, a pair of Frenchmen, are known to have survived. They reached Anosy and one was eventually rescued by one of the first French ships to visit southern Madagascar. Robert Drury also reports the story of a French ship wrecked at Fenambosy in Mahafaly country two or three years before the wreck of the *Degrave* in 1703. He heard that there were no survivors from the massacre of its crew.

The only European foothold in the south was the tiny French colony at Fort Dauphin. The colonists here lived through a series of events from 1642 to 1655 in which relations with their Tanosy neighbours degenerated from an *entente cordiale* to all-out war. When the Portuguese had landed at Ranofotsy Bay a century earlier, they had marked the spot with a marble pillar; such marks of 'ownership' were carried from Europe by the exploring ships of the Portuguese and erected wherever they touched land. Flacourt had the Portuguese monument re-inscribed with the French royal coat of arms (the three fleurs-de-lis) and with a Latin text giving the date it was inscribed, and commemorating Louis XIV and himself. On the lower part of the stele was written:

O ADVENA LEGE
MONITA NOSTRA
TIBITVIS VITÆQ-
TVÆ PROFVTVRA
CAVE AB INCOLIS
VALE

Latin was the European educated classes' secret language, understood regardless of nationality. Even when nation was at war against nation or in competitive trading relationships, it was still part of a common bond between Europeans that reminded them that, whatever their differences, they were in this together. The Malagasy 'natives' were the outsiders. The translation reads:

OH NEWCOMER
READ OUR ADVICE
IT WILL BE USEFUL FOR YOU, YOURS AND YOUR LIFE
BEWARE OF THE INHABITANTS
FAREWELL

Flacourt was so pleased with his inscription that he even drew himself a picture of the stone.

Flacourt left for France in 1655 and in 1656 a new governor named Champmargou arrived to take charge of the colony. He found that the fort had been burnt in a Tanosy attack, that Pronis the old governor was dead, and two *roandria* had been executed in retaliation. Champmargou was a military man who had neither Pronis's local connections nor Flacourt's feel for the politics of the region. His policies of attack and confrontation left the colony wholly alienated from its hinterland. All that saved him were the abilities of his remarkable second-in-command. Le Rochelais Le Vacher, who became known as La Case, sounds like a real-life version of the Kurtz of Conrad's *Heart of Darkness* and Coppola's *Apocalypse Now*. This extraordinary Frenchman worked out how to live successfully in southern Madagascar. La Case lived in his own Tanosy village, well away from Fort Dauphin and the inflexible governor, and often led his band of Tanosy warriors on missions against the Mahafaly. He evidently realised that marriage was the key to becoming accepted in Malagasy society and his successful move was to marry the daughter of a *roandria* of the Tanosy royal clan and thereby enter the complex system of alliances which were the basis for political and social life.

La Case's local knowledge bailed out Champmargou many times. He even saved his life when the zealous governor had walked himself into trouble. A missionary priest had insulted a local *roandria* by condemning him for having more than one wife and had thrown the man's sacred talisman into a fire. The priest had been killed for his actions and in consequence Champmargou led a punitive force against the *roandria*, unaware that he was leading his men into an ambush. La Case's warriors arrived just in time to prevent the *roandria's* six thousand men annihilating the French troops.

During the 1660s more colonists and soldiers were sent to Fort Dauphin from France. Yet the colony was no more productive than before and many died from disease and in combat. By 1672 La Case and governor Champmargou were both dead and the Sun King, Louis XIV, was advised that Fort Dauphin should be abandoned. The uninhabited island of Réunion looked like a much better prospect for an Indian Ocean colony and a small contingent of just two hundred settlers was left to sink or swim in Madagascar. The end of the embattled colony came in 1674 after a series of heart-breaking events involving a boatload of brides.

A group of girls had been shipped out from a French orphanage, bound for Bourbon (Réunion) where they were to wed the island's settlers. Their ship called in at Fort Dauphin to unload much-needed supplies for the dying colony. As it was leaving the bay, it hit a shoal and sank. The women were all brought ashore, and to extricate themselves from what must have seemed a precarious situation they begged the colony's governor that they might marry some of his colonists. One sees their point – they were heading to the ends of the earth, to unknown husbands on an unknown island, so why risk the perils of the sea any further? The Fort Dauphin men were probably as good as any others in the girls' opinion.

The governor agreed, quite unaware of the likely consequences. Of course, all the Fort Dauphin colonists were living with Tanosy wives – the governor himself was married to La Case's half-Tanosy daughter (even though the child was barely twelve years old) – but the requisite number of men was selected and a mass wedding was arranged. The Malagasy women were packed off home to their villages. What the French did not realise was that their marriage alliances with their Tanosy neighbours were all that had kept them hanging on. This severing of family ties was tantamount to declaring war. On 27 August 1674 the outraged Tanosy attacked. Two-thirds of the settlers were massacred. By great luck another ship arrived in the nick of time and, thirteen days later, the survivors spiked the fort's guns, burnt the remaining stores and headed for Réunion. One has to hope that the orphan girls made it to safety but no one knows – some of them were last heard of stranded in Mozambique! After thirty years of death and disaster the French sailed away for good, leaving behind more than four thousand of their countrymen and an unknown number of Malagasy buried in the forests of Anosy.

Looking back on the two hundred years of European disasters in southern Madagascar before Drury arrived, it would have taken a miracle to avert the *Degrave* massacre. Like our own entanglements with the frightened and hostile Tandroy, the *Degrave* incident was part of a history of unhappy encounters between the Europeans and the Malagasy. Misunderstandings and betrayals led to two centuries of massacre and conflict. The Tandroy may not have been directly involved in many of the incidents, but news of the foreigners would have travelled faster than the traded guns and powder which could be obtained from these Europeans. The fate of the *Degrave*'s crew may not have been inevitable but it had built up from a series of threats, hostage-takings and fighting which had occurred with depressing regularity in so many colonial encounters throughout the south. It was just a little bit more human blood spilt in the hot sand of southern Madagascar.

Rescue Arrives

Drury may have thought that the west coast was a place of safety but this illusion was soon shattered. There was another war in the wind and this time Drury's luck ran out. He was on the losing side. The Fiherenana army had allied itself with the Tandroy in common cause against the Mahafaly and now the Mahafaly got the upper hand. They sought their revenge by attacking the Fiherenana from the south while the army of the expanding Sakalava kingdom swept down from the north. The Sakalava were a terrible enemy: their kingdom had long been trading for guns with the outside world and they were probably better armed than anyone else in Madagascar. Trapped in this pincer movement, the Fiherenana forces fought a desperate running battle.

Drury and his West African friend were in the thick of the fighting. They fell behind their fellows and, although they tried to hide from the enemy in a cane thicket, they were soon spotted. The African was shot dead and Drury was captured. Although he was soon licking the feet of a new master, Drury was surprisingly unworried about falling back into slavery. He had worked out that he might wait years before a ship called at St Augustine – most of the traders and pirates were using ports much further north, in Sakalava country, so he was happy to be heading off with the Sakalava army.

Mahabo, the capital of the Sakalava, was over 200 miles north of St Augustine, about 20 miles inland on the Morondava river, and it was here that Drury first saw his new monarch, King Ratsimonongarivo. At the edge of the town the royal court sat in state, waiting to greet the returning warriors who sounded conch-shell horns in acclaim. Even here in this great kingdom there was no palace and no throne – like the Tandroy leaders, the king sat on a simple mat. The eighty-year-old Ratsimonongarivo was 'a very odd, and formidable Figure', dressed in an ornate style Drury had never seen before.

The king's hair was arranged in layers of plaits, with gold and glass beads knotted into the tresses. Necklaces covered the old man's shoulders and he wore heavy silver bracelets and gold rings on his fingers. His legs were adorned with twisted strings of beads and he was wrapped in two silk *lamba*, one around his waist and another on his shoulders. Drury was vastly impressed by the king's principal wife, the fattest woman he had ever seen in his life. Her breasts hung down to her lap and she could barely walk, being carried on a litter wherever she went.

Drury observed the new world into which the fortunes of war had brought him. He had no trouble with the language, apart from slight variations in dialect and pronunciation, but some things were different. The houses of important men were much bigger than those of the Tandroy, being 24ft long by 18ft wide, and were constructed from wooden planks. The land in which he now lived was much less arid than Androy; the Sakalava kept huge herds of cattle and grew rice in their fields.

Drury's new master Revovy was a grandson of the king. This young man treated Drury well, reckoning that since foreigners had no home to return to in Madagascar, they would always stay where they were best looked after. Drury, by now about twenty-five years old, was given a prestigious position as captain of Revovy's guard, commensurate with his exotic foreign origins, and soon realised that he was going to be well cared for, with plenty to eat and drink. His main duty was to keep an eye on his master's wife, not so much to protect her as to prevent any dalliances with other men. As it turned out, it was Revovy himself, 'a gallant young Man, addicted to his Pleasures and some Vices', who had a wandering eye and Drury got embroiled in his master's 'Love-Adventures'.

One day Revovy decided to take his household on a tour of the north to inspect his cattle and during this journey Drury met some of the most enigmatic people in Madagascar's history, the Vazimba. He was informed that these were the original inhabitants of Madagascar but he could not tell how one might know. The spirits and the memory of the vanished Vazimba are still honoured in Madagascar today although almost nothing is known about these mysterious people who are thought to have been the descendants of the very first settlers of the island. The description in *Robert Drury's Journal* is one of the few eye-witness accounts of what they looked like and how they lived.

Although Drury sees many similarities between the Sakalava and the Tandroy, when he describes the Vazimba he seems struck by differences. These people even spoke a different language which he could not understand. The backs of their heads and their foreheads were 'almost as flat as a Trencher', probably a deliberate deformation caused by head-binding.

Vazimba food was wonderful. Despite all his years in Madagascar Drury had never really taken to the local fare and comments that during his stay with the Vazimba he ate some of the most agreeable meals of his life. Even their pots were so different that Drury thought them worth describing: they were made by 'glazing them both within, and without'. It sounds as if the Vazimba were still using an ancient style of graphite-burnished wares. These had been common throughout Madagascar in Flacourt's time in the seventeenth century, but Drury would never have seen the style because it had become outmoded by his day.

Already living with the Sakalava when Drury turned up were several other captured outsiders and castaways. He first met Lewis, a black Jamaican sailor who had made his way north after being stranded at St Augustine's Bay when his ship was captured by pirates. Unknown to Drury, this same Lewis had already encountered another Androy castaway. Captain Drummond, who had escaped from the massacre in 1703, is said to have wandered miserably in Madagascar until he was eventually murdered somewhere in the west – by a Jamaican named Lewis. In the royal capital of Mahabo there lived a Portuguese from the East Indies called Francisco. Francisco too had been set ashore by pirates and now worked as a carpenter. He had every intention of staying with the Sakalava because he was 'violently in Love with a young Woman'. Sadly, the girl later jilted him.

King Ratsimonongarivo was also looking after an English youth named William Thornbury who had gone ashore from his ship with two shipmates to find provisions, only to see their ship sail away without them. His companions had died soon after and Will had now spent about nine years with the Sakalava, who had never tried to treat him as a slave. Will had got by in relative comfort compared to Drury's experiences at the hands of the Tandroy, whom the Sakalava regarded as 'the worst of Brutes in that unpolish'd Country'. Drury also met two emissaries from 'Amboerlambo' (*amboalambo* or 'dog-pigs', an insulting name for the highland Merina). They were ambassadors to the Sakalava court from the mountain kingdom of Imerina and explained to Drury that their landlocked country had trouble procuring the guns that coastal people such as the Sakalava were able to obtain from trading with passing ships.

A few months after meeting the Merina ambassadors, Drury missed his first chance for rescue. In 1714 an English ship, the *Clapham*, commanded by Captain Wilks, arrived on the coast to trade for slaves along the Morondava river. William Thornbury was allowed to take this chance to go home but Revovy would not let Drury go. Consumed with his desire to leave, poor Drury tried to communicate his plight to Captain Wilks. He wrote a message on a leaf and sent a runner to take this improvised letter the 60 miles downriver to the ship. Of course, the messenger dropped it. Not knowing that it was the writing that was important rather than the leaf, the messenger did his best by substituting another, more impressive piece of foliage. Its recipient on the *Clapham* must have been quite baffled.

After this incident Drury decided to flee to a new master: Revovy's uncle Remomy, who was 'a Man of a great deal of good Nature, and Humanity', and lived a lot nearer the coast, so Drury would have a better chance to hear of incoming ships. Although crippled from the waist down and unable to walk, Remomy was still 'a very Great Prince, and extremely well-belov'd' by his people and his twelve wives. Drury spent another two-and-a-half years in Remomy's company, long enough for Remomy to suggest that Drury needed a wife. His master found him a suitable woman but Drury says very little about her. Perhaps he never felt the way he had about the girl he left behind in Androy. They were happy years with the Sakalava and, apart from wanting to see his parents once more, Drury really had no inclination to try to get back to England. He had a herd of cattle of his own and lived 'in Affluence and Ease'.

Then one day, the postman came. There was a letter for Drury. It was from William Mackett, the captain of an English slave ship called the *Drake*. He wrote to send word that his ship anchored off the nearby coast had on board not only a letter from Drury's father but instructions to purchase Drury's liberty. William Thornbury, who had sailed to freedom more than two years before, had almost forgotten Drury – but not quite. One day soon after his return to London, he went to the pub. Sitting over a beer in the Crown in Rotherhithe, he overheard the men in the next booth talking about someone lost in Madagascar. Will had run into Robert's younger brother John. Thanks to Will's information, Captain Mackett was on the lookout for the stranded Englishman.

The kindly Remomy gave Drury permission to depart and with the prince's blessing he left the next day for the coast. There were two ships in the bay, Mackett's *Drake* and another called the *Sarah*. Drury found the ship's shore party but had awful trouble making them understand who he was. He had difficulty speaking English and the slave traders thought this half-naked figure with long matted hair and sunburnt skin was some sort of a 'wild Man'.

When it dawned on the *Drake*'s men that they had found their castaway, they promptly tried to turn this Tandroy warrior into an Englishman, cutting his hair, shaving him and dressing him in sailor's clothes. After years wearing only a *lamba* and living among a people who decorated their hair with plaits and beads, Drury was thrust back into a world of wool and wigs. He had a big adjustment to make: European men's clothing consisted of a long 'vest' or waistcoat, a long, full-skirted coat and breeches to just below the knee, the origin of the modern suit. Men's hats, known as 'beavers', were large with wide brims folded upwards, prefiguring the three-cornered cocked hat. Perhaps the strangest item of attire was the wig. These were made from human, horse or goat hair and even, at the bottom of the range, wool, with many variations in size and shape: shorter tied-back wigs were worn for travel and work, and even labourers might wear one.

Poor Drury must have been wildly uncomfortable being back in breeches for the first time in thirteen years and he was soon extremely ill from the change of diet. Once recovered, he sailed upriver aboard the *Sarah* to his old home to meet Remomy and buy slaves.

Back at the coast after this successful expedition, a third ship arrived. This was the *Mercury*, under Captain Thomas White, a slave trader formerly working the West African coast. In October 1715 he had obtained a licence from the East India Company to sail to south-east Africa and Madagascar for whaling, ivory (called 'elephants' teeth' at the time) and 'other commodities' – the euphemism for slaves. As well as the *Drake*, the *Mercury* and the *Sarah*, this slaving expedition included another ship named the *Henry*; a fifth little vessel under the command of Mackett's brother accompanied the *Mercury*.

The *Henry* had lagged behind its companions, so Captain Mackett's fleet waited around the north-west coast for this last vessel to come in and then dispersed on the hunt for good business. In early October 1716 Drury set sail on board the *Drake* to the port of Massalege (also spelt Masselege, near present-day Mahajanga). In this northern province of the Sakalava he was part of an expedition inland to a royal village. The fisherman who guided the shore party told Drury that they would find four white men from Ile Sainte Marie living there. Drury does not say whether these men ever let on to Mackett's party about their occupation but he certainly knew what they were – pirates.

When the men from the *Drake* arrived at the village the chief was away at war, but his principal wife greeted the strangers and along came two of the pirates. Drury was feeling pretty edgy around these men and cocked his guns, ready for trouble. One of them was a Dutchman, dressed in a short coat with plate-buttons and sporting a sash in which he had tucked a pair of pistols. He was also holding a pistol in his hand. The other was similarly equipped with intimidating weaponry, but Drury realised he knew the man. They had been boys together on the *Degrave*.

He was Nick Dove, one of the young midshipmen who had been spared after the massacre at the sand hill. Many years earlier he had run away from his captors in Androy and reached Fort Dauphin. After two years there he had gone by canoe to Matatana whence he had been picked up by a pirate ship operating out of Ile Sainte Marie. Nick had lived for a while on the pirate island until one day his new shipmates had sailed their elderly vessel to the mainland where they had constructed a small fort, armed with the ship's cannon, under the command of a former ship's carpenter, the pirate Tom Collins.

During nine years of living in a state of perpetual war with the local tribes, the besieged men had built themselves a new ship. Collins and others had decided to stay at the east coast fort but a breakaway faction – which included the Dutchman John Pro, Nick Dove and the notorious pirates Burgess and Zachary – had sailed their little sloop around Madagascar's north coast and settled down here in Sakalava country. Pro now had a fine house furnished with pewter plates, chests to sit on and a real bed with curtains. He also owned many cattle and several slaves.

Nick had heard that John Benbow had got home to England and that Drummond had died in Madagascar, though where, when and how he did not know. Neither he nor Drury knew that other survivors from the *Degrave* had been in Massalege before them. Sometime in 1704 some of the group of men who had sloped off before the massacre and made it to the east coast had seized a passing ship and sailed to Massalege, where they fell in with the pirates. Other stragglers were found in St Augustine by pirates in 1706. All these men had faced a deathly choice – once in Madagascar, almost the only way to leave was by joining a pirate ship. It is unlikely any of them ever made it back to England.

Captain Mackett probably couldn't care less whether the four men in the Sakalava village were pirates or not. What was he supposed to do about it? The crew all remained with them until the chief returned from war. Only once he was back could they buy the slaves that he had for sale. During the dealings of slaves for guns this chief gave a twelve-year-old girl to Drury, who had no compunction in immediately selling her to John Pro.

By early January the ships had full complements of slaves. It was time to head for the Atlantic. On 20 January 1717 Drury said farewell to Madagascar – nearly sixteen years after leaving London, he was finally on his way home. But his troubles were not yet over. The long voyage to England was a perilous adventure in itself. After leaving Madagascar the *Drake* sailed without stopping to St Helena. This little rock in the south Atlantic had been settled in 1659 by the East India Company to provide a provisioning station for the Atlantic voyage, and here Mackett intended to sell some of his human cargo. The bill of sale still survives in the records of the Company's St Helena factory.

When the high surf abated enough for the crew to unload, the *Drake* would offer for sale four little children under the age of twelve, two boys and two girls aged between twelve and seventeen years, four women and six men, all said to be able-bodied and in good health, although the captives had been aboard for at least two months and Drury says some of them were sick by now. If this first batch of slaves was snapped up, they would sell another set.

It seems incomprehensible that Drury could bear this part of the job: he spoke the language of these children, he had lived since boyhood with men and women such as these but appears to have had no feelings at all about seeing them sold, facing an early death far from home. He never mentions the least qualm of conscience. On 11 March the ship took on three barrels of gunpowder and on 16 March Captain Mackett left St Helena with a note of hand for the huge sum of £869 18s 8d for the slaves purchased on credit by the island's planters. Slaves were certainly a valuable cargo.

The *Drake* sailed on to Barbados and then to Jamaica to deliver the rest of the enslaved Malagasy in her hold, arriving in Port Royal on 6 May. There Captain Candler of the warship HMS *Winchelsea* noted in his log for that day the arrival of 'Capt. Maggett from Maddigascar'. After a two-month layover the *Drake* sailed for home on 5 July in a convoy of twenty-eight ships bound for England under the protection of the *Winchelsea*. But even the last leg of Drury's journey was not without incident.

Within a week the convoy had been scattered by wind and currents and they had pirates on their tail. In spite of the presence of the warship, the merchantmen were attacked by two ships under the pirate captain Hornigold. The *Drake* saw them off with broadsides from her sixteen guns. The pirate ships headed into shallower water where they were safe from pursuit by the 40-gun *Winchelsea* and then under cover of darkness they slipped away, still managing to rob two of the vulnerable merchantmen which had fallen behind.

The last mishap was a collision on 22 July between the *Drake* and the *Winchelsea* which left both ships badly damaged. They made repairs at a nearby island and on 27 July HMS *Winchelsea* turned back and left the convoy to make the rest of the voyage across the Atlantic unescorted. On 8 September the *Drake* and four other ships reached the

Downs. On 13 September 1717 they were back at Gravesend, where Drury's adventures had begun.

Robert Drury must have wondered on that homeward voyage what on earth was going to happen to him now. He was to find that his home and family had changed beyond recognition: his mother had died years ago, in 1703; his father had left the King's Head, remarried, and retired to Loughborough in Leicestershire, where Robert had a half-sister he had never met. His old home, the King's Head, had been taken on by his uncle, William Drury, but William too was dead and the inn was being run by his aunt Margaret, who had already lost a second husband. His sister Elizabeth too was already a widow, but on the point of marrying for a second time. His little brother John had been nine years old when he last saw him – he was now a grown man of twenty-six, working as a baker in London. Drury arrived too late to see his father again – after sending into the unknown that letter to his lost son in Madagascar, John Drury had died in 1716.

Robert Drury was thirty years old, had spent most of his life as a Malagasy and had come back to a world he could barely remember. He had no money and no profession. He did not belong in the urban bustle of London and yet he had spent so many years trying to escape from the only adult life he knew back in Madagascar. Perhaps he saw no option for survival other than to go back to sea and use his strange skills and experience in the slave trade.

The Slave Turns Slaver

The London to which Drury returned had expanded, filling up with the rural poor. Bad harvests during the 1690s followed by the enclosure of common land had driven people into the towns and cities, especially the capital. The city was becoming ever more divided in terms of class and money. The rich and the social climbers inhabited the spacious new houses of the West End, providing work for a small army of service trades – tailors, wig-makers, porters and prostitutes. Many of the brothels were concentrated in the area around Covent Garden and in the inner West End parishes.

In 1700 John Brown described London as a city of cheats and drunkards living in the seething bustle of streets filled with hawkers and porters, carts and sedan chairs, weaving around the barrowboys and their wheelbarrows full of nuts. The roads and waterways of London were clogged with traffic and the air itself was choking both indoors and out, full of smoke from coal fires and tobacco fumes.

For the writer-publican Ned Ward, London was a colourful world of taverns and bawdy houses full of jilts and bumsitters, trulls and muckworms, smoking, drinking and gambling the night away. A lot of people spent a lot of their time drunk, but then business did take place in ale-houses and coffee-houses. Life in the streets was noisy, crowded and sordid, but not all London's denizens were lechers, thieves and drunks – the vast majority were hard-working and respectable citizens.

The country to which Drury returned even bore a new name – it was the United Kingdom now. Wales had earlier been assimilated into a union with England in which the Welsh were very much the junior partners, sneered at by the English as stupid and poverty-stricken, speaking their own language in the 'fag-end of Creation'. The union of Scotland and England had taken place during Drury's absence.

Back in London, Drury must have felt far from home and exactly a year later, on 13 September 1718, he left England again on board Captain White's ship, the *Mercury*. White and Mackett had applied to the East India Company for another trading licence and now they were off again to Madagascar for more of those 'other commodities'. It was not the best season to sail and the *Mercury* took nearly seven months to get to the Cape of Good Hope.

Cape Town in the early 1700s was a little colony of several hundred whitewashed stone houses with attractive gardens. Opposite the church a large hospital, built in the plan of a cross surrounded by a moat and a wall, had room for five hundred patients. Six army surgeons worked with black slaves to tend the continuous stream off the passing ships of sick seamen suffering from scurvy, dysentery, malaria and other illnesses. As the Dutch colonist Johan Buttner observed, every day two or three dead sailors were carried out of the hospital to be buried.

Malagasy captives, along with others from Angola and elsewhere, were brought in by slavers and housed in a large stone courtyard building known as the Logie. Johan Buttner noticed that the children of the enslaved girls were fair-skinned, fathered by the European men who passed through the colony.

On 29 April 1719 the *Mercury* anchored off Natal where White dropped off six Africans who had accompanied him on the earlier voyage, supplying them with enough provisions for the long walk home to their native country of Mozambique. Captain White hadn't been entirely honourable towards his African passengers – two princes from the Mozambique coast had happily gone aboard his ship expecting to be taken to see England but he had sold them as slaves in Jamaica!

Trading began here in southern Africa and White soon purchased seventy-four children in return for large brass rings and other goods. The next stop was Madagascar. Drury went ashore at Fort Dauphin and set off to the royal capital to buy slaves. He was there taken aback to find that the king was dressed in a coat and breeches and wearing a hat. Conversely Drury had changed back into Malagasy dress and was wearing a *lamba* and sporting a spear. The king explained that he hated the French – they had killed his grandfather and taken an uncle captive – but still found other Europeans acceptable to trade with. On 20 July the *Mercury* unloaded the children bought in Natal and left them under guard in Fort Dauphin while the ship went on up the east coast to pick up more slaves in Matatana. Captain Mackett's ship was ahead of them – they knew that he had been in Matatana just three weeks earlier and had bought a huge cargo of 330 slaves.

Drury was detailed to spend time ashore in Matatana negotiating for slaves while the *Mercury* made a side-trip to the French colony on the island of Réunion to see if there was any good business there. Drury stored his stock of slaves behind the defences of the royal village, unhappy about the danger from warring neighbours which threatened to overrun this small kingdom. The ship arrived back to fetch them in mid-September, under a new captain. Thomas White had died suddenly and the ship's new commander was George Christal.

Drury's new slaves were brought by canoe through the surf to the ship, which then set sail back to Fort Dauphin. On putting in there, the slavers discovered that Anosy was in turmoil. During their brief absence the king had been killed in battle and confusion reigned. The situation was volatile and the Tanosy were in no condition to trade, so the men of the *Mercury* hastily took the child-slaves from Natal back on board and sailed westwards along the coast of Androy. Drury remains silent on how he felt. He had been ashore on the east coast for nearly three months, living among the Tandroy's near neighbours, and one wonders if he had asked for news of the people who had been not only his captors but the family and friends of his youth. Now he saw again the very spot on which the *Degrave* had sunk all those years ago.

The next port of call was Morondava, where Drury certainly heard news of his Sakalava acquaintances. The *Mercury* anchored on 16 October and the new captain and his ship's musicians accompanied Drury inland to Mahabo. They learnt that old King Ratsimonongarivo had died and Drury's former master Remomy now ruled as monarch. Remomy had not forgotten his red slave. Ever since Drury's departure nearly two years earlier, Remomy had looked after Drury's little herd for him. Still a cattle man at heart, Drury went and clipped his new calves' ears with his personal mark. Within ten weeks the ship was loaded with slaves and on 7 January 1720 Robert Drury said his last farewell to Madagascar.

The *Mercury* is recorded as calling at the Cape on 4 February, although Drury does not mention it. He does remember putting in to St Helena on 7 March, where the ship had been contracted to deliver some slaves: eleven men and five women. They left St Helena to a fifteen-gun salute from the garrison and made their way across the Atlantic to Barbados and then to the Rappahannack river in Virginia, where they traded the rest of their slaves for a cargo of tobacco. The *Mercury* arrived back in the Downs on 11 September 1720, at the end of Drury's last known voyage.

Robert Drury's involvement in the enslavement of his fellow human beings is utterly reprehensible. Yet in both the countries in which he lived, Madagascar and Britain, slavery was morally acceptable. For the Malagasy, prisoners of war had always provided manual labour. After the Merina kingdom pacified most of Madagascar in the nineteenth century, the supply of prisoners dried up and as a consequence the Merina imported slaves from Africa until 1877. Slavery was not abolished in Madagascar until 1896.

For the British in the 1700s, selling people for money was big business. Like most businesses, it had investors, brokers and competitors – and no morals: the British 'purchased that with their money which nobody ought to sell, and dealt in those commodities, to get money, which it's a pity anybody should buy'.

The Royal African Company specialised in exporting people from West Africa to the Americas. It was founded in 1672, with a licence to trade for a thousand years. By 1700 about 106,000 Africans had been shipped across the Atlantic by the company; up to a fifth of them died during the crossing. The trade was so lucrative that the Royal African Company had trouble hanging on to its early advantages. Interlopers encroached: the company lost its legal monopoly and Bristol overtook London as Europe's main West Indies harbour. Smaller slaving businesses operated out of the little ports of Devon and the south coast. For many people the sleepy seaside towns of Falmouth, Lyme Regis and Weymouth may be the innocent places of childhood holidays – but these and others like them prospered and grew on the profits of slavery.

Eighteenth-century England had some ground to make up in the slavery business. In 1444 the Portuguese had started carrying captured Africans to Europe as slaves and the Spanish and Portuguese had been stocking their colonies with thousands of slaves since the early 1500s. They showed no signs of letting up: there were Portuguese sugar plantations in Brazil and Spanish *haciendas* in Hispaniola, Cuba and Mexico producing sugar, cattle and tobacco and in need of labour. This was also the time of the first gold rush. In 1698 gold had been found in Minas Gerais in Brazil. Initially the Portuguese had forced the native Indians into the mines, but eventually, captured Africans were imported as more gold was discovered. An estimated 150,000 Africans were carried to Brazil in the ten years after 1700, their labour used to prop up the decaying empire of the once-dominant Portuguese. Direct routes between Rio and Africa were opened up and just such a slave-buying journey from Brazil to Africa was used by Daniel Defoe as the setting for the shipwreck at the start of Robinson Crusoe's adventures.

The *asiento* – the monopoly contract for trading slaves into Spanish territories in the New World – was a prize to be sought and in 1713 the English won it from the French. England was already a more important slaving nation than

France, importing an estimated hundred thousand slaves to its colonies of Jamaica and Barbados between 1700 and 1710, in contrast to half these numbers working on the French slave plantations in the Caribbean.

In North America the English colonists transformed their own society into a militarily aggressive, slave-based economy. In Virginia the colonists had been farming tobacco since they landed in 1607 and developed the plantation system before the arrival of enslaved Africans – the first are recorded in 1619 – but slavery and the transition from family farms to plantation estates really took off in the fifty years before 1700, by which time there were over ten thousand slaves working the plantations. In Carolina, a colony founded only in 1670, the British settlers made their living out of slaving, deerskins, cattle-raising and, after its introduction from Madagascar in the 1690s, rice. Production of this labour-intensive crop stimulated both the import of African slaves and slaving raids on Indian villages. In 1700 the Carolinians began the first of three Indian wars, sending thousands of Native American captives to work and die on the sugar plantations in the West Indies. In 1704 the Governor of Carolina estimated that more than half of Carolina's total population of 9,580 were slaves, African and Native American.

Since Cromwellian times radical groups such as the Levellers had expressed beliefs about the equality and freedom of all men, and yet few in English society spoke out against the slave trade. Indeed, attitudes hardened during the late 1600s and the anguished pleas, made mainly by churchmen, against the inhumanity of slavery were muffled by an acceptance of the economic gains to be made. During the late 1690s the English philosopher John Locke wrote treatises on tolerance and freedom, yet was himself deeply implicated in slavery, not only buying shares in the Royal African Company but taking an active hand in the governance of Britain's slave plantations. Sir Isaac Newton, remembered as a hero for his scientific achievements, was also quite a businessman. He had been made Master of the Mint in 1699 and had overseen a scheme to reform the coinage – milled coins were issued, not amenable to clipping for their silver content. There were now more than £7 million worth of these brand-new coins in circulation, greasing the wheels of trade and commerce.

Alongside this worthy work for capitalism, Newton tried to profit personally from the trade in human lives by investing heavily in the South Sea Company which obtained the *asiento* contract. One of the commercial aims of this company was therefore to buy and sell people: 4,800 slaves a year would be bought in Africa and shipped over to Jamaica, where the weak ones would be 'eliminated', and then on to the Spanish ports in the Caribbean and South America. When the South Sea Company's bubble burst and the company went bust in 1720, nine years after it was founded, the investors got their morally deserved come-uppance. Newton himself lost £20,000 – about £20 million in today's money.

England had the largest merchant marine fleet in Europe and a business community trading all over the world. Most of Britain's imports, worth over £3 million a year, and a similar amount of exports were handled through London, where there were over twenty docks and thirty repair yards for ships between Blackwall and Southwark. The interconnections between North America, the Caribbean, West Africa, India and the Far East all centred on London and its merchants. England was poised to become the world power, militarily triumphant and at the centre of a global commercial empire. The coming together of economic dominance, the philosophies of 'rationalism' and a taste for luxuries needed one more piece in the jigsaw. If some of the new sources of wealth were tobacco, sugar and coffee, who was to provide them? Even the most Christian Englishmen considered slave-trading to be the answer, as long as the slaves were well treated. Nobody fought to put an end to the human suffering which enriched the English and other Europeans. Trade conquered all.

A vehement champion of slavery and one of the leading lights behind the South Sea Company's foundation was Daniel Defoe. Writing in 1713 he pointed out that without enslaved

Africans there was no sugar, and without sugar there was ultimately no trade. As he saw it, the African trade was the key to the whole commercial system and also potentially the most profitable investment of all. Yet the export trade to Europe was still the most significant generator of capital in England, even greater than the African slave trade or the trade with America and the East Indies. Our slave traders could have made a good living a lot closer to home.

The mystery remains of how Robert Drury could bear to go slaving, knowing from bitter experience the misery of being a captive far from home. Drury was part of the slave trade in the western Indian Ocean, one of the areas of the world for which we have much evidence for the long history of human bondage. The peoples of East Africa, referred to in early documents as the Zanj, had been the prey of Arab slavers for centuries; thousands were shipped from ports such as Zanzibar to the kingdoms around the Persian Gulf and to labour on the task of draining the swamps of southern Iraq. The Chinese historian Chou Ch'ü-fei, writing in AD 1178, describes the purchase by the Chinese of thousands of slaves from Zanzibar. He calls some of them *K'un-lun-Ts'eng-Chi* or 'Malays at the ends of the earth in the country of the blacks' – a reasonable description of the Indonesian-descended people of Madagascar and probably the earliest reference to the slave trade from that island.

European explorers reported on the trade in slaves from Madagascar in the sixteenth century. The Portuguese admiral Tristan da Cunha visited the north-west in 1506 and found small towns where Arabs came to trade for slaves, rice and wax. In 1521 the Turkish admiral Piri Re'is reported that the people of the Comoros, a little archipelago 300 miles north-west of Madagascar, 'raised' slaves for export. The precise scale of Arab and Chinese slave-trading in the Indian Ocean is hotly debated. For some it is a phenomenon almost equivalent to the later European trade; other historians claim it was just a trickle in contrast to the more barbarous European involvement. Cairo was certainly importing about twelve hundred slaves a year when Arab slaving was still in full swing, and one estimate suggests that Arab slavers of the seventeenth century took about ten thousand mostly female captives from sub-Saharan Africa to the Orient.

The first Europeans to muscle in on the Arabs' export business from Madagascar were the Portuguese, who started trading for slaves directly with the kings of the north-west coast and buying them second-hand from Arab middlemen. The Dutch were next on the scene, arriving in about 1623 on the lookout for a cheap workforce for their colonies on Mauritius and in the East Indies. From the seventeenth and eighteenth centuries the French and English had joined the trade and we have detailed information about the scale of the enterprise.

In the period between 1675 and 1725 about twelve thousand Malagasy were taken to the Americas. In the 1680s and 1690s a Dutch-American trader named Frederick Philipse shipped Malagasy captives into Manhattan and the first recorded slaves in New Jersey arrived in 1683 from Madagascar. The long haul from the Indian Ocean was, however, considered too expensive in money and lives for it ever to have been a major element of the Atlantic trade. Mortality of crew and captives was higher than on any other route and the slave traders were not too keen on the Malagasy as either cargo or workforce since they considered them less robust than Africans. The South Carolinians were an exception – they valued Malagasy slaves because of their ability to cultivate rice.

Recently, archaeologists have excavated a small part of the African Burial Ground in New York which was in use from the end of the seventeenth century until 1794. As many as twenty thousand people were interred here and DNA tests on some of the skeletons indicate that about 3 per cent of them were Malagasy – perhaps about six hundred individuals in the entire cemetery. Many people in North America today will have Malagasy ancestors who arrived there three hundred years ago.

The main destinations for Malagasy captives were Java, Cape Town, St Helena and the islands of Mauritius and

Réunion which were in constant need of fresh imports, not only because so many slaves died there, but also because many escaped to live in freedom in the forests or made themselves canoes and sailed home to Madagascar. Slaves sold to St Helena were not so lucky, since there was nowhere to hide and no escape from the island.

The pirate community of Madagascar was definitely involved in slaving – the bid for liberty and equality made by these Europeans and Americans did not extend to the Malagasy. Captain Burgess, one of the pirates whom Drury met in Massalege, was a middle-man, shipping slaves along the short coastal route from St Augustine up to the Arab depots on Madagascar's north-west coast. Captain Plantain sold Malagasy captives to the English at Bristol and the Dutch at Batavia (now Jakarta), while other pirates supplied New York and Martinique.

Before 1700 the main slaving areas were Madagascar's north-west and north-east coasts, with isolated southern ports at St Augustine and Fort Dauphin, but soon other ports of the south-east, particularly Matatana where Drury collected a cargo of slaves, also became key areas. The South Sea Company knew that their Spanish customers preferred dark-skinned Malagasy from the coast and the south, not 'the tawny sort with straight hair' from the highlands. The impact of the trade was colossal.

Madagascar's petty kingdoms had been locked in endemic conflict since well before the coming of the Europeans, but the trade in slaves led to more sustained wars fuelled by the need to capture as many people as possible and by the growing demand for guns. Political survival depended on maintaining the balance between cornering the trade in guns and not overly antagonising powerful neighbours by enslaving too many of their subjects.

Although the Tandroy had a large slave population, they seem never to have been heavily involved in the trade. Their most valued commodity was cattle, to be exchanged for guns with the Tanosy. The rise in weaponry was extraordinary. In 1650, at the beginning of this arms race, the Tanosy possessed nine muskets. In 1768–9 alone the French brought for trade to Fort Dauphin 10,000 guns, 100,000 pounds of powder, 120,000 musket balls and 300,000 gunflints. In Drury's time a slave was worth one musket. Sixty years later the Europeans were trading two or three guns for one slave. When the Tandroy were finally subdued by the French colonisers, the number of their guns (most of them ancient muskets) confiscated by 1904 was estimated at between twelve and sixteen thousand.

Robert Drury was a minor player caught up in one of the most explosive periods in Madagascar's history. Sometimes a victim, sometimes an agent of enslavement and warfare, his adventures took him to the furthest reaches of the European colonial world and deep into the human misery that comes from wrenching people from their homeland and sending them to early deaths from disease and brutal treatment. Drury was both English and Malagasy at the same time, a Cockney Tandroy fully belonging to neither society, yet the two worlds in which he spent his life had something quite unexpected in common – neither society would have condemned him for becoming a slave trader. Slavery was one of the facts of life, ingrained in Drury's view of the world. It makes him a disappointing hero for the modern reader: one's pity for the slave merges into loathing for the slaver.

An Illiterate Scribbler?

On 24 May 1729, some twelve years after Drury's return to England, a book relating all his adventures was published in London: *Madagascar: or, Robert Drury's Journal, during Fifteen Years Captivity on that Island*. The abbreviated title, *Robert Drury's Journal*, encapsulates two crucial problems with his book. Firstly, is it a 'journal'? A journal is a continuously updated, usually daily, account of events. But Robert Drury's 'journal' was written many years after the adventures it describes. Even though today we have photographs and films to prick our memories, how accurately does anyone at the age of forty-one remember the details of what happened to them when they were only thirteen or fourteen? Secondly, is it Robert Drury's own work? In the preface to the first edition an anonymous editor tells us that the original *was* written by Robert Drury and consisted of eight folio-sized quires, each of nearly a hundred pages, so that the editor's job had been merely to contract it and 'put it in a more agreeable Method'. Yet from the story told in the book, we learn that during his years of captivity Drury almost lost the ability to speak English, let alone to write it fluently. Could he have produced 'his' journal unaided?

Warning bells sound when we read the *Journal*'s preface: 'I make no Doubt of its being taken for such another Romance as "Robinson Cruso"' and 'it is nothing else but a plain, honest Narrative of Matter of Fact'. Here are traces of the greatest novelist of his day, an embroiderer of the truth who assumed many identities to tell his stories. Daniel Defoe lurks in the shadows behind this book.

In that time of great beginnings and new worlds, the first novels were being written. The earliest English novel was written by a woman, Aphra Behn, in 1688. *Oroonoko* is the story of a West African prince taken into bondage and transported to Surinam where he escapes from slavery with his princess lover, kills her in a death pact and finally dies horribly at the hands of his English captors. Not only was it a realist novel, pretending to tell a 'true' story, but it was also the first literary exposé of the horrors of slavery.

Like Behn, Daniel Defoe used rhetorical devices in his novels to create an atmosphere of 'reality' and included a rich background of detail. Undoubtedly, Behn and Defoe based their stories on aspects of the truth – Behn almost certainly spent some years in Surinam while Defoe's inspiration for *Robinson Crusoe* was the true story of the castaway Alexander Selkirk. Curiously enough, both Behn and Defoe were employed as spies in their earlier years and both knew how to tap a rich vein of fantasy to enliven a framework of raw facts. Yet the defining characteristic of these early novels is that they address contemporary and very real political concerns.

Neither Oroonoko nor Crusoe ever existed but here, in the innovative form of the novel, was a powerful technique to win hearts and minds to favourite causes. Defoe was an activist for the Whigs, who heartily approved of slavery and hated Roman Catholics. At the same time he vociferously upheld freedom from religious persecution, being himself a Dissenter, one of a minority of nonconformist Protestants who faced much discrimination in political and social life. Most importantly, Defoe was a champion of the importance of English trade and colonisation.

In *The Life and Strange Surprizing Adventures of Robinson Crusoe* Defoe created a foundation myth for the new colonialism and capitalism – the enlightened, rational and modern Englishman, supported by his Christian God, domesticates nature and establishes an idealised colony with its sole representative of the subject races, the affable Man Friday. Published in 1719 when Defoe was about fifty-nine, and written in an exciting and popular style (by eighteenth-century standards), the book was a runaway success. It went through forty-one editions in forty years and remains the most famous adventure story ever written.

Surprisingly, we know less about Daniel Defoe's early life than about Robert Drury's. He was the son of Alice and James Foe, probably born in the autumn of 1660, perhaps in Cripplegate, London. His father was a tallow chandler wealthy enough to send him away to school in Dorking and then to a Dissenters' school, Charles Morton's Academy in Newington Green. These provided a good education but they were not Eton and Oxford, perhaps explaining why Defoe never mixed with the *literati* of his day. His contemporaries such as Alexander Pope, John Dryden and Jonathan Swift were, frankly, out of his class socially, as well as being on the opposite side of a deep political and religious divide. Swift once snidely referred to Defoe as 'an illiterate scribbler'.

In 1684 Daniel married Mary Tuffley, who was to bear him eight children, of whom four daughters and two sons survived infancy. In the first year of his marriage Defoe probably left home to fight for his beliefs. He is known to have received a royal pardon in 1687, which implies that he had been an active combatant on the losing side during a Protestant rebellion in 1685. He supported the Duke of Monmouth, Charles II's doomed bastard son, against the Catholic James II's forces at Sedgemoor in Somerset, in the last battle ever fought on English soil. Defoe welcomed the new Protestant monarchy in 1688.

In that year Defoe started publishing pamphlets on economic ideas and some fairly radical politics, as well as getting involved in a number of business ventures. Mary's dowry had provided him with a small fortune of £3,700 which he squandered on fruitless enterprises. He was a brilliant pamphleteer but a hopeless businessman. After trying and failing to make a profit as an importer, he fell into debt, was declared bankrupt in 1692, and was briefly imprisoned owing the immense sum of £17,000. Defoe's ideas about how to make a fortune then went from bad to lunatic. He bought a diving bell, with the intention of looking for sunken treasure off the Scilly Isles. He bought seventy civet cats, hoping to make money from their anal glands (which provided one of the base constituents of perfume). Nothing worked and he was to remain on the run from his creditors for the rest of his life. One of them even pursued him after his death, hoping to get some of his books and possessions as a return on the £800 that she had lent him in 1691, forty years earlier.

Our best physical description of Defoe comes from a 'wanted' poster of 1703: 'He is a middle-sized spare man, about forty years old, of a brown complexion, and dark brown-coloured hair, but wears a wig; a hooked nose, a sharp chin, grey eyes and a large mole near his mouth.' He was also referred to as Daniel de Foe, alias Daniel de Fooe. This advertisement for his arrest was published in the wake of his ironic pamphlet *The Shortest Way with Dissenters*. In a parody of fierce Tory views, Defoe recommended systematic extermination as the answer to religious problems! He had made the politicians look stupid and, after coming out of hiding, he ended up in the pillory, but was cheered by the crowds rather than pelted with bricks and stones. He was then sent to Newgate prison.

Out of prison again (and bankrupt again), in 1704 Defoe launched the *Review*, a lively newspaper of comment aimed at his own people: the tradesmen, the Dissenters and the urban middle class. It even had a problem page in which he played agony aunt, answering readers' questions on the difficulties of courtship and marriage. Defoe was an independent thinker, a chameleon of a writer who had the ability to outrage his own side as well as his opponents and, although a success in journalism, he was treated as a pariah by his peers.

Manipulated by political patrons, Defoe in turn manipulated the readership of the journals for which he wrote, able to argue convincingly on any side of the major questions of the day. Not everyone appreciated the irony of some of his articles and his challenging writing on politics ensured him a third spell in prison in 1713. In 1725 Defoe underwent an excruciatingly painful operation for bladder stones. The method sounds appalling: the patient was strapped to a board and cut open between anus and scrotum for insertion of a catheter to remove the stones – and all without any anaesthetic. He was a partial invalid after this experience but was writing better than ever.

Defoe's period of novel writing had already come to end – he wrote all his novels in the space of just five years, between 1719 and 1724 – but a host of essays under the pseudonym Andrew Moreton appeared around this time. The pen was his weapon to propagate his views on the world, attack his enemies and defend his corner. By 1726 he had published the broadly non-fictional *Tour of the Whole Island of Great Britain* and *The Complete English Tradesman*. For Defoe the distinction between truth and fiction was not clear-cut and he regularly employed his journalistic tricks to mix fiction with fact to tell a more entertaining story.

Until 1729 Defoe lived in the London suburb village of Stoke Newington but his money problems were getting out of hand. He had to disappear to escape his creditors. Now sixty-five years old and on the run once again, he moved to near Greenwich and then found a hiding-place in central London. He was so broke by now that he couldn't even pay the rates on the family's home in Stoke Newington. He died of 'lethargy' (probably a stroke) on 24 April 1731 in lodgings in Rope-Maker's Alley and his death was registered in St Giles's Church, Cripplegate, in the parish where he was born seventy-one years earlier. His body was buried in the Dissenters' cemetery at Bunhill Fields, Finsbury. A tombstone was carved for him in 1870 and can be seen today in Hackney Museum.

With *Robinson Crusoe*, Daniel Defoe had tapped into a subject which enthralled the reading public of the day. Although Defoe himself never left Britain, like many others of his generation he was fascinated by the distant and exotic world from which people were bringing back extraordinary tales. So Robert Drury's stories of his adventures in Madagascar were published to an interested audience eager to learn about faraway lands and peoples. For the next 150 years there seems to have been no question that *Robert Drury's Journal* was indeed what it purported to be. And then in 1872 a first doubt was expressed. The Frenchman Emile Blanchard indicated his disbelief: would the Malagasy truly have dared enslave a European? Such a question could only come from a point of view of enormous cultural arrogance, but in the 1890s more serious questions were raised as to the truthfulness of the account and some began to suspect that Defoe was having a last laugh.

Defoe revolutionised travel writing by concentrating on the practical and psychological experiences of the individual. Stories of adventure could be told from a fictional personality's perspective rather than from the lofty distance of a detached commentator. He enjoyed leading his audience on, sprinkling his novels with truths to mislead the reader and inserting fictional elements into his non-fiction. During the twentieth century a number of critics began to argue that Defoe was not simply the anonymous editor who had clearly knocked *Robert Drury's Journal* into shape but the sole author, employing the notion of a fictitious 'editor' as a literary device. A scholar named John Robert Moore was the most vociferous advocate of this theory, claiming that many turns of phrase in the *Journal* could be matched to sentences in known writings of Defoe. The book was dismissed as another of Defoe's fireside travels. Defoe's own private library was sold after his death and the sale catalogue is a useful document since we can find out what Defoe owned and read – but, although it includes a couple of his own later works, there is no copy of *Robert Drury's Journal*.

Is there any concrete evidence that can link Defoe to Drury? What was Drury doing during the years between his return to England and the publication of the book? Some scholars argue that the first trace of Drury after his return in 1720 from his slaving expedition suggests the possibility that the paths of the two men may have crossed. His father's will had left Robert with £200 and various heirlooms – if his brother and sisters died childless, he was to have his mother's wedding ring and his father's quill pen and silver watch. He also inherited a share in a house in Stoke Newington, the village where Defoe was living. In 1721 Robert and his brother John appeared before Stoke Newington's manorial court to relinquish their rights to this property, but there is no proof that Robert ever lived in Stoke Newington.

There is another place where Defoe and Drury might have met. In the final paragraph of his book, Drury announces that he is available to answer questions and can be found at Old Tom's Coffee-House in Birchin Lane in the City of London. This coffee-house was well known as a depot for books and periodicals, some of them by Defoe, a journalist who garnered details for many of his books by seeking interviews with people who had useful first-hand information. Perhaps he spent time in the coffee-house listening to Drury droning on to the assembled company with his stories about 'When I was in Madagascar . . .'. Old Tom's is long gone but you can still get a cup of coffee in Birchin Lane today.

Drury reappears once more in the records of the East India Company. The Court Minutes of 18 March 1729 recorded:

> Request of Robert Drury being read representing he had lived on the island of Madagascar 15 years, that he has now an offer of returning thither in the Sweeds service but will not engage in it if the Company have any objection thereto, or that they will be pleased to afford him an employ in their service whereby he may be able to get a decent livelihood.

Robert Drury's Journal appeared in May of the same year, prefaced by an affidavit from Captain William Mackett, dated 7 May 1728, confirming that he did indeed bring Drury back from Madagascar and that the story was 'genuine and authentick'. Some have seen this as another literary trick, used to persuade the reader of the veracity of a possibly bogus story. Statements about 'truth' are common prologues to such texts as the Indian captivity stories from seventeenth-century North

America and the American slave narratives of the late eighteenth and nineteenth centuries.

Is that affidavit a fake or not? Although Drury drops out of sight between 1721 and 1729, we do know something about William Mackett. He was a wealthy and influential figure, well known in London's shipping circles, who certainly made two further voyages for the East India Company, one on the *Nightingale*, which he lost at the Cape in 1722, and the second on the *Princess of Wales* in 1726–8. He died in the spring of 1729, just weeks before *Robert Drury's Journal* was first published. Some literary critics have suggested that Daniel Defoe would have been quite capable of concocting a convincing affidavit and that Mackett's death was just what Defoe needed – the captain's timely demise meant he couldn't object if his name was used on a false authentication. But if Mackett really had no part at all in the story of Robert Drury, Defoe would have been taking a terrible risk – the captain's name is used in the chapters of the book describing the rescue from the west coast as well as on the affidavit. If Defoe chose Mackett's name at random – any old dead Company captain would suit his purposes – he would have had to have written the whole of the end of the book in a space of days and would still have had to face the likelihood that any of Mackett's acquaintances could expose the lie.

We know little more about Drury's life back in London after his final voyage to Madagascar. According to the contemporary writer William Duncombe, Drury was well known as a porter at East India House in Leadenhall Street and lived in a house in Lincoln's Inn Fields. He was renowned for having become expert at throwing the 'javelin' while in Madagascar. He seems never to have married. The last news of Robert Drury is, of course, his death. On 15 March 1733 he was buried in the churchyard of St Clement Danes near Lincoln's Inn Fields. He was only forty-five years old.

The Unfinished Story

If Daniel Defoe did have a hand in *Robert Drury's Journal*, how can the grains of truth be sifted from the chaff of his manipulations and falsities? The most important breakthrough in deciding how to treat *Robert Drury's Journal* – true or false, fact or fiction or a bit of both – came in the 1950s. The American literary academic Arthur Secord did some marvellous detective work. All he had to go on was the name 'Robert Drury' – the ordinary name of an ordinary man whom most of Secord's colleagues thought was probably fictional. But Secord found him. He not only established the details of Drury's life but also discovered in archives the independent testimonies of John Benbow and Robert Coleson. These demonstrated for the first time that the events on the *Degrave* up to and including the massacre did indeed happen.

In spite of this, the debate about Robert Drury's story continues. Most recently Anne Molet-Sauvaget, a French historian, has attributed the book to Defoe. She points out that, like other works by him, it is said to be based on an original but vanished manuscript written by a person who really existed. Both are devices used by Defoe in other works. The first half of the book, describing the voyage from Bengal, the shipwreck and the escape from Fenoarivo, varies in style from the rest of the book and may derive from a different source. Molet-Sauvaget suggests that it could come from the account of John Benbow who died in 1708 – his lost manuscript is a possible source for all the events described up to the night before the massacre.

As for the content of the rest of Drury's book, the details of his life in Androy, Molet-Sauvaget's own research has confirmed much detail that could only have been known to someone who had had close contact with the Tandroy. The people Drury names in the book are real.

Some critics think that the answer to this question of authorship lies elsewhere – that Drury did spend a very short time in Androy but that he was back in England by 1705, the 'little boy' picked up on St Helena by the *Raper*. As a consequence of this theory, the latter part of Drury's story describing his years of captivity as a slave is seen as pure fiction, spinning out the tale as far as it would go. Yet Drury would have been seventeen in 1705, not a 'little boy', and this explanation still does not solve the literary critics' problem – who wrote the book?

There are some very good reasons why Defoe was *not* the author of the *Journal*. He was undeniably interested in Madagascar, but the *Journal* does not have Defoe's rumbustious style and the book is sometimes rambling, full of detail which certainly the modern reader can find quite dull. If this is a novel, then the narrative structure is desperately weak as the story fizzles out long before the end of the book – rather more like real life than fiction! If the first part of the narrative – the really good bit – is Drury or Benbow's story, and the second half is entirely a work of Daniel Defoe's imagination, why did a writer of his calibre not liven it up to make a more exciting read?

The fourth edition of Drury's book was published in 1743, ten years after his death, under the variant title of *The Pleasant, and Surprizing Adventures of Mr. Robert Drury, during his Fifteen Years Captivity on the Island of Madagascar*. A note on its last page states that during conversations with the late author at Old Tom's Coffee-House 'several inquisitive Gentlemen have receiv'd from his own Mouth the Confirmation of those Particulars which seem'd dubious, or carried with them the least Air of a Romance'. Who added this footnote, and made many changes to the text? Even if Daniel Defoe were the book's editor, these cannot be his words since he too was long dead. There is a third hand at work here. Who would bother to keep up the pretence after the deaths of both Defoe and Drury? It seems more likely that someone, perhaps Robert's brother or sister, wanted to insist on the story's authenticity.

Literary critics wrestle incessantly with the strange genre of 'travel fiction' and, because *Robert Drury's Journal* has much in common with other works of its period, they have tied themselves in knots trying to disprove the 'truth' of the text. We decided to look at Robert Drury's story from another perspective, from Androy itself. The more we have found out about the Tandroy past and present, the more we realise that to have written such a convincing book someone must have spent a long time out there in southern Madagascar. Of course, we have to accept that Defoe wrote much non-fiction, especially in his later years, and that attribution to Defoe does not revolve solely around the question of truth versus fantasy.

Looking carefully at the *Journal*, there are signs of a rather heavy-handed editor responsible for insertions and digressions in the story. For example, a short treatise on the theory of government (a recurring theme in the works of Defoe) interrupts an anecdote, dividing it into disjointed sections. The narrator occasionally muses on the difference between 'reason' and 'superstition', and there is also much philosophising about Providence. Such ruminations on the nature of belief and religion may well be those of a Dissenter (like Defoe) and not an Anglican (as Drury had been baptised).

There were undoubtedly many writers in London in 1729 who would have been capable of giving book-length treatment to Drury's story in the literary manner pioneered by Defoe, but how many of them were Dissenters and how many would have played the anonymity game – who would have *not* wanted their name to appear on a book? We can never prove whether Defoe was involved in *Robert Drury's Journal* or to what extent. Our best guess is that he was, but only as editor and transcriber, not as author of the whole tale.

Robert Drury's Journal was never a wildly popular story and has rarely been republished. There are clear reasons why it never achieved the fame of *Robinson Crusoe*. Some of these are literary: it is not written particularly well and does not have a spectacularly exciting plot. Other reasons concern its social impact. In *Robinson Crusoe* Defoe created a myth of colonial destiny: like much of his writing it is propaganda, aimed at influencing and encouraging the small but affluent minority which was constructing capitalism in England. *Robinson Crusoe* is a colonialist tract, with reason triumphing over nature and over other cultures – a manifesto for Britain's imperial glory and technological progress. *Robert Drury's Journal* is quite the opposite. It is about British sailors who simply want to go home.

Even if the shipwrecked crew of the *Degrave* had any ambitions towards colonisation, these are simply not relevant, since the Tandroy were not prepared to be subjugated. The Tandroy were far from being barbarians; they were instead initially most hospitable, taking in the crew on their own terms. The British start out with technological superiority but lose horribly to the Tandroy. Robert Drury comes to admire many aspects of Tandroy culture and even tells us that they ultimately showed him more love and kindness than he ever knew among the English.

Many of these aspects of the story are fully exploited by the editor. If that editor was Daniel Defoe, then in this book he certainly turns the searchlight back on his own society in a style very different from *Robinson Crusoe*. *Robert Drury's Journal* is a subversive book because its world is one turned upside-down. The white man is the slave. The concept of Christianity is made to look ridiculous. The savages are actually more human than the civilised. Ultimately, Drury is not a spokesman for a powerful culture overwhelming all in its path but one of the little people whose views and experiences differed hugely from those of his more chauvinistic and self-confident contemporaries. He is, by the end, almost more Malagasy than he is English. So it is no wonder that the book became largely forgotten. It expresses ideas that undermine the ideology of colonial expansion and world domination – hardly suitable fodder for Drury's contemporaries involved in commercial enterprise and, later on, definitely not an instructive model for the Victorians intent on building their empire.

As for Tandroy appreciation of the Drury story, it has little if any relevance in southern Madagascar today. He was just one of many thousands who were enslaved in the past. There seems to be no memory of him or of the *Degrave* which sank on the shores of Androy. Such tales of minor incidents in the past have no purpose and no place in Tandroy oral traditions and would have been soon forgotten, eased into oblivion by more relevant and powerful stories about the noble ancestors. In a similar way, *Robert Drury's Journal* has also been forgotten in Britain, pushed aside by the mythically powerful *Robinson Crusoe*. Yet texts can be dusted off and rediscovered whereas oral traditions, once lost, can never be resuscitated.

We can close *Robert Drury's Journal*, but the tale resists any ending. Our version of Drury's adventures is neither a search for the absolute truth of his book nor simply a 'whodunnit' mystery – to find out if Defoe murdered Drury's story and how he did it. It has also been a journey of discovery in several directions.

Robert Drury's life reveals something of how the world has come to be as it is today and, in particular, the long history of the relationship between the western world and a people like the Tandroy who live far away from Europe and America. The Malagasy themselves express quiet misgivings about that relationship and puzzle over how the western world perceives them and their country: why do we spend so much money conserving their island's wildlife when so little is invested in the human inhabitants? Perhaps we care more about animals and plants than we do about people?

We have tried to unravel Drury's story with the aid of a group of people with a culture very different from our own. All the Tandroy whom we have met during our fieldwork, even those who distrusted us, know that their history is of more than local interest. Just as in Britain, some people may be baffled – and very amused – about why we bother to pick up broken pots and dig holes in windswept sand dunes, but at least we have been able to say why we think Androy is important. Like many societies outside Europe, the Tandroy have conventionally been considered to have no worthwhile 'history' of their own, but they have helped us step through a door into their ancient past.

Bibliography

Only the more easily accessible literature and most important sources are listed here. A full bibliography is available on line at
http://www.shef.ac.uk/~ap/research/madagascar/robert_drury

Robert Drury: His Life and His Journal

Drury, R., *Madagascar: or, Robert Drury's Journal, during Fifteen Years Captivity on that Island*, London, W. Meadows, 1729.

——, *The Pleasant, and Surprizing Adventures of Mr. Robert Drury, during his Fifteen Years Captivity on the Island of Madagascar*, 4th edn, London, W. Meadows, 1743 [1729].

East India Company, *Marine Records* L/MAR/A/CLIX [the muster-roll of the *Degrave*] and *Court Minutes,* vol. 53 (1730), 444 [Drury's request to return to Madagascar].

Molet-Sauvaget, A., *'Madagascar ou le Journal de Robert Drury' par Daniel Defoe*, Paris, Harmattan, 1992.

Parker Pearson, M., 'Reassessing *Robert Drury's Journal* as a historical source for southern Madagascar', *History in Africa* (1996) 23, 233–56.

Secord, A.W., 'Robert Drury and *Robert Drury's Journal*', *Notes and Queries* (1945) 189, 178–80.

——, 'Defoe and *Robert Drury's Journal*', *Journal of English and Germanic Philology* (1945) 44, 66–73.

——, *Robert Drury's Journal and Other Studies*, Urbana, Illinois University Press, 1962.

Pirates

Cordingly, D., *Life Among the Pirates: the Romance and the Reality*, London, Little, Brown and Co., 1995.

Cordingly, D. (ed.), *Pirates: an Illustrated History of Privateers, Buccaneers, and Pirates from the Sixteenth Century to the Present*, London, Salamander Books, 1996.

Cordingly, D. and Falconer, J., *Pirates: Fact and Fiction*, London, Collins and Brown, 1992.

Deschamps, H., *Les Pirates à Madagascar aux XVIIe et XVIIIe Siècles*, Paris, Editions Berger-Levrault, 1972.

Jameson, J.F. (ed.), *Privateering and Piracy in the Colonial Period: Illustrative Documents*, New York, Augustus M. Kelley, 1970 [1923].

Johnson, C. (Daniel Defoe), *A General History of the Robberies and Murders of the Most Notorious Pyrates* and *The History of the Pyrates*, ed. M. Schonhorn, London, J.M. Dent and Sons, 1972 [1724 and 1728].

Molet-Sauvaget, A., 'Un Européen, roi "légitime" de Fort-Dauphin au XVIIIe siècle: le pirate Abraham Samuel', *Etudes Océan Indien* (1997) 23/24, 211–21.

Rediker, M., *Between the Devil and the Deep Blue Sea: Merchant Seamen,*

Pirates and the Anglo-American Maritime World, 1700–1750, Cambridge, Cambridge University Press, 1987.

Ritchie, R.C., *Captain Kidd and the War Against the Pirates*, Cambridge MA, Harvard University Press, 1986.

The Early History of Madagascar

Allibert, C. (ed.), 'Autour d'Etienne de Flacourt (Actes du Colloque d'Orléans)', *Etudes Océan Indien*, 1997, 23/24.

Brown, M., *A History of Madagascar*, London, Damien Tunnacliffe, 1995.

Dewar, R. and Wright, H.T., 'The culture history of Madagascar', *Journal of World Prehistory* (1994) 7, 417–66.

Flacourt, E. de, *Histoire de la Grande Isle Madagascar*, ed. C. Allibert. Paris, INALCO and Karthala, 1995 [1661].

Kent, R.K., *Early Kingdoms in Madagascar 1500–1700*, New York, Holt, Rinehart and Winston, 1970.

Kottak, C.P., Rakotoarisoa, J.-A., Southall, A. and Vérin, P., *Madagascar: Society and History*, Durham NC, Carolina Academic Press, 1986.

Parker Pearson, M., 'Close encounters of the worst kind: Malagasy resistance and colonial disasters in southern Madagascar', *World Archaeology* (1997) 28, 393–417.

Reade, J. (ed.), *The Indian Ocean in Antiquity*, London and New York, Kegan Paul International/British Museum, 1996.

Vérin, P., *Madagascar*, 3rd edn, Paris, Karthala, 1990.

Ships, Sailors and Trade

Bruijn, J.R. and Gaastra, F.S. (eds), *Ships, Sailors, and Spices: East India Companies and their Shipping in the 16th, 17th and 18th Centuries*, Amsterdam, Neha, 1993.

Chaudhuri, K.N., *Asia Before Europe: Economy and Civilization of the Indian Ocean from the Rise of Islam to 1750*, Cambridge, Cambridge University Press, 1990.

Earle, P., *Sailors: English Merchant Seamen 1650–1775*, London, Methuen, 1998.

Keay, J., *The Honourable Company: a History of the English East India Company*, London, HarperCollins, 1991.

Lawson, P., *The East India Company: a History*, London, Longman, 1993.

Sutton, J., *Lords of the East: the East India Company and its Ships*, London, Conway Maritime Press, 1981.

Britain in 1700

Davison, L., Hitchcock, T., Keirn T. and Shoemaker R.B. (eds), *Stilling the Grumbling Hive: the Response to Social and Economic Problems in England, 1689–1750*, Stroud, Sutton, 1992.

Drummond, J.C. and Wilbraham, A., *The Englishman's Food: a History of Five Centuries of English Diet*, London, Jonathan Cape, 1939 [quoted in chapter 9].

Earle, P., *A City Full of People: Men and Women of London 1650–1750*, London, Methuen, 1994.

Linebaugh, P., *The London Hanged: Crime and Civil Society in the Eighteenth Century*, London, Allen Lane, 1991.

O'Gorman, F., *The Long Eighteenth Century: British Political and Social History 1688–1832*, London, Arnold, 1997.

Speck, W.A., *The Birth of Britain: a New Nation 1700–1710*, Oxford, Blackwell,

1994.

Thomas, K., *Religion and the Decline of Magic: Studies in Popular Beliefs in Sixteenth- and Seventeenth-Century England*, London, Weidenfeld and Nicolson, 1971.

Ward, E., *The London Spy*, ed. P. Hyland, East Lansing, Colleagues Press, 1993 [1709] [quoted in chapter 2].

Wolf, E.R., *Europe and the People Without History*, Berkeley, University of California Press, 1982.

Androy and its People

Decary, R., *L'Androy (Extrême Sud de Madagascar): Essai de Monographie Regionale*, vols I and II. Paris, Société d'Edition Géographique, Maritime et Coloniale, 1930 and 1933.

——, *La Mort et les Coutumes Funéraires à Madagascar*, Paris, Maisonneuve et Larose, 1962.

Defoort, E., *L'Androy: Essai de Monographie*, Antananarivo, Bulletin Economique, 1913.

Heurtebize, G., *Histoire des Afomarolahy (Extrême-Sud de Madagascar)*, Paris, CNRS, 1986.

——, *Mariage et Deuil dans l'Extrême-Sud de Madagascar*, Paris, Harmattan, 1997.

Mack, J., *Madagascar, Island of the Ancestors*, London, British Museum Publications Ltd, 1986.

Middleton, K., 'Who killed "Malagasy cactus"? Science, environment and colonialism in southern Madagascar (1924–1930)', *Journal of Southern African Studies* (1999) 25, 215–48.

Parker Pearson, M., 'Matérialité et rituel: l'origine des tombeaux en pierre du sud de Madagascar', *Anthropologie et Sociétés* (1999) 23, 21–47.

——, 'Eating money: a study in the ethnoarchaeology of food', *Archaeological Dialogues* (2000) 7, 217–32.

Rajaonarimanana, N. and Fee S., *Dictionnaire Malgache Dialectal – Français: Dialecte Tandroy*, Paris, Langues et Mondes/L'Asiathèque, 1996.

The Archaeology of Southern Madagascar

Heurtebize, G. and Vérin, P., 'Premières découvertes sur l'ancienne culture de l'intérieur de l'Androy (Madagascar): archéologie de la vallée du Lambomaty sur la haute Manambovo', *Journal de la Société des Africanistes* (1974) 44, 113–21.

Parker Pearson, M., 'Tombs and monumentality in southern Madagascar: preliminary results of the central Androy survey', *Antiquity* (1992) 66, 941–8.

——, 'Qui étaient les Ampatos? L'archéologie des développements politiques du XVe au XVIIIe siècle en Androy', *Etudes Océan Indien* (1997) 23/24, 237–52.

Parker Pearson, M., Godden, K., Ramilisonina, Retsihisatse, Schwenninger, J.-L. and Smith, H., 'Lost kingdoms: oral histories, travellers' tales and archaeology in southern Madagascar', in P. Funari, M. Hall and S. Jones (eds), *Historical Archaeology: Back from the Edge*, London, Routledge, 1999, 233–54.

Parker Pearson, M., Ramilisonina and Retsihisatse, 'Ancestors, forests and ancient settlements: Tandroy readings of the archaeological past', in P. Ucko and R. Layton (eds), *The Archaeology and Anthropology of Landscape: Shaping your Landscape*, London, Routledge, 1999, 397–410.

Radimilahy, C., *L'Ancienne Métallurgie du Fer à Madagascar*, Oxford, BAR

Supplementary Series 422, 1988.

Vérin, P. and Heurtebize, G., 'La trañovato de l'Anosy: première construction érigée par des Européens à Madagascar: descriptions et problèmes', *Taloha* (1974), 6, 117–42.

Flora and Fauna, including Giant Birds

Anderson, A., *Prodigious Birds: Moas and Moa-hunting in Prehistoric New Zealand*, Cambridge, Cambridge University Press, 1989.

Fuller, E., *Extinct Birds*, New York, Viking/Rainbird, 1987.

Goodman, S.M. and Patterson, B.D. (eds), *Natural Change and Human Impact in Madagascar*, Washington DC, Smithsonian Institution Press, 1997.

Jolly, A., *A World like our Own: Man and Nature in Madagascar*, New Haven, Yale University Press, 1980.

——, *Lemurs and Lords, Mad Scientists and Men with Spears*, in press.

The Slave Trade

Campbell, G., 'Madagascar and the slave trade 1810–1895', *Journal of African History* (1981) 22, 203–27.

Manning, P., *Slavery and African Life: Occidental, Oriental, and African Slave Trades*, Cambridge, Cambridge University Press, 1990.

Thomas, H., *The Slave Trade: the History of the Atlantic Slave Trade 1440–1870*, New York, Simon and Schuster, 1997.

Daniel Defoe and Early Travel Writing

Adams, P.G., *Travelers and Travel Liars 1660–1800*, Berkeley and Los Angeles, University of California Press, 1962.

——, *Travel Literature and the Evolution of the Novel*, Lexington, University of Kentucky Press, 1983.

Baine, R.M., 'Daniel Defoe and *Robert Drury's Journal*', *Texas Studies in Literature and Language* (1974) 16, 479–91.

Furbank, P.N. and Owens, W.R., *The Canonization of Daniel Defoe*, New Haven, Yale University Press, 1988.

——, *Defoe De-Attributions: a Critique of J.R. Moore's Checklist*, London, Hambledon Press, 1995.

Moore, J.R., *Defoe in the Pillory*, Bloomington, Indiana University Press, 1939.

——, *Defoe's Sources for* Robert Drury's Journal, Bloomington, Indiana University Publications, Humanities Series 9, 1943.

——, 'Further notes on Defoe's sources for *Robert Drury's Journal*', *Notes and Queries* (1945) 188, 268–71.

Todd, J., *The Secret Life of Aphra Behn*, London, André Deutsch, 1996.

Guide Book

Bradt, H., *Guide to Madagascar*, 7th edn, Chalfont St Peter, Buckinghamshire, Bradt Publications, 2002 [1988].

Index